MODERN

SOUTHWEST

CUISINE

MODERN

SOUTHWEST

CUISINE

John Rivera Sedlar

with Norman Kolpas

Photographs by Richard Clark

Photographs Styled by Cheryl Branter

TEN SPEED PRESS
Berkeley, California

Ten Speed Press
P.O. Box 7123
Berkeley, California 94707

Cover Design by Fifth Street Design, Berkeley, California
Book Design by Karolina Harris
Illustrations by Glenn Wolff
Book Production directed by Richard L. Willet

Manufactured in the Republic of Korea
1 2 3 4 5 — 98 97 96 95 94

Library of Congress Cataloging-in-Publication Data
Sedlar, John, 1954—
    Modern Southwest Cuisine / John Rivera Sedlar with
Norman Kolpas ; photographs by Richard Clark ;
photographs by Cheryl Branter.
        p.   cm.
Originally published: New York : Simon and Schuster,
c1986
Includes Index.
ISBN 0-89815-650-5 : $19.95
ISBN 0-89815-640-8 : $24.95
    1. Cookery, American—Southwestern style.
    I. Title.
TX715.2.S69S44   1994
641.5979—dc20   94-26556
                                    CIP

Acknowledgments

First and foremost, I must thank my partner, Steve Garcia, for sharing with me a vision of a restaurant that became Saint Estèphe, and for his unyielding dedication to our restaurant, his impeccable palate for fine wines, his sense of fairness and his generous and professional collaboration in the development of Modern Southwest Cuisine.

My mom and dad, Rose and Joe Sedlar, blessed me with two very different but complementary views of the world. With my dad, our family traveled throughout Europe and the United States, and I was exposed to a broad variety of cultures. Through my mom, I was steeped in the rich Hispanic civilization of the American Southwest. Together, these two influences have culminated in the development of my cuisine.

Special thanks go to my grandma, Eloisa Rivera, who has served as the culinary link between my family's Southwestern ancestors and my own modern style of cooking. Many of the dishes in this book found their inspiration in the kitchen of Grandma Eloisa, and she continues to inspire me to this day.

My buddy Norman Kolpas undoubtedly contributed the most to the completion of this book. His unparalleled professionalism and good-natured humor made burning the midnight oil effortless and gratifying. Thanks, Norman.

Carole Lalli, my editor at Simon & Schuster, showed great faith and enthusiasm in this project.

Photographer Richard Clark, with his meticulous professionalism, helped me to create a unique look for this book.

Cheryl Brantner began her involvement with Saint Estèphe by designing all of the graphics for the restaurant. Her creative vision found special expression in the art direction for the photographs in this book.

Mary-Ann Parshall served as food stylist for the photography.

Philip Garaway, of the Native American Art Gallery in Venice, California, generously lended me native Southwestern art from his extensive collection for use in the photographs.

Susan Grode deserves thanks for her guidance in making all arrangements for the book's publication.

Joe and Siria Garcia have been the spiritual parents of Saint Estèphe—without them, the restaurant would not have been possible.

Ann Kennedy and Janet Brownley have, from the beginning, been two of the staunchest supporters of Saint Estèphe.

Rickie and Morris Montoya of Josie's Best in Santa Fe, New Mexico, were the first Southwestern food suppliers to ship their products—including blue cornmeal and blue corn tortillas—to Saint Estèphe. They work hard with me to develop new products for the restaurant.

Mary Yoon and her gourmet chocolate shop Entiché du Chocolat make all of the custom chocolates for Saint Estèphe. Mary is unflagging in the enthusiasm and expertise she brings to developing all new chocolate ideas for the restaurant.

Susan Wiseman was invaluable in helping me organize such major events as the opening night party for the Maya Exhibition at the Los Angeles County Natural History Museum and our special dinner for Roger Vergé. Susan also helped greatly in organizing and preparing the food for photography in this book.

Glenn Robarge, from the kitchen of Saint Estèphe, helped me in the complex organization and preparation of food for the photographs, and he was of invaluable assistance in keeping things running smoothly in the restaurant.

A number of people believed in Saint Estèphe from the very start, and their support of the restaurant was instrumental in our growth—including Andrea and Pula Garcia, Angelo and Lucille Garcia, Leroy and Barbara Garcia, Delores Garcia, Anita and Richard Lopez, Margaret Rogers, Salomon Garcia, Murray Granard, Jerry Newsome, Berry Barbour, Frank Agosto, and Tom and Lisa Hutchinson.

Fred Hoffman made the stencils and some of the chocolate molds used at Saint Estèphe.

Pam Gardener helped me with the initial proposal for this book. Her continued faith in the project has meant a great deal to me.

Gail Rico, who keeps Saint Estèphe's books, is greatly valued for her friendship and help.

Bill Safarik has been a friend and helper of Saint Estèphe from the beginning.

For their continued support and friendship, I would like to thank Tim and Rose Martella and Josh and Linda Fredricks.

This book is dedicated
to the Hispanic people and Pueblo Indians of northern New Mexico

Contents

CHAPTER 3
APPETIZERS

CHAPTER 4
SALADS

Introduction

In developing a Modern Southwest Cuisine, I have combined the traditional ingredients and the kitchen vernacular of American Southwestern cooking with the techniques and sensibilities of modern (or *nouvelle*) French cuisine. The idea of such a combination surprises many people. Frankly, they wonder if the two really go together—whether the earthy simplicity of Southwestern cooking can make a happy, stable marriage with the aristocratic refinement of the French kitchen.

I believe they can. This book was written while I was still at Saint Estèphe restaurant. The food I served at that restaurant grew out of my own experiences as a native of the American Southwest, a classically trained chef and, most importantly, as a person who loves good food. I left Saint Estèphe in 1990, but many of the culinary styles I developed there have been carried onto the menus of restaurant Bikini, in Santa Monica, and restaurant Abiquiu, in San Francisco. Modern Southwest Cuisine is a natural development of my heritage and my profession. And as I learn more about the traditional foods and flavors of the Southwest and new ways to cook them, my cuisine continues to grow and evolve.

Memories of Southwestern Cooking

I was born in Santa Fe, New Mexico. My father was in the Air Force, and during my childhood we lived all over the United States and in Spain and France. But every few years, we came home to Santa Fe. And whenever we came home, my mother's people would gather together to welcome us.

Often the gatherings would take place in Abiquiu, thirty-five miles northwest of Santa Fe, at the home of my Great-Uncle Gabriele and Great-Aunt Corina—the adobe home originally built by my great-grandparents Eloy and Pablita Martinez. Happy, robust women filled the kitchen as they rolled tortillas, steamed tamales and fried sopaipillas for lunch and dinner. The smell of hot oil, the aroma from simmering pots brimming with pinto beans, the taste of fresh tortillas cooked over a wood stove—in spite of my travels, these are my earliest memories of good eating.

My grandma Eloisa Rivera was and still is a wonderful cook. In the fall, when zucchini and corn were at their sweetest and most plentiful, she'd make heaping pots of a mixed vegetable dish called *calabacitas*—"little squashes." She gathered

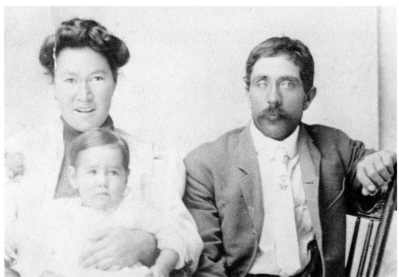

My great-grandparents, Pablita and Eloy Martinez, with my great-aunt Rafaelita

apricots from her sister Corina and brother-in-law Gabriele's orchards and put up preserves that lasted the whole year. At Christmas, hundreds of *bizcochitos*, little anise-flavored cookies, and the fried mincemeat pies called *empanaditas*, would come out of Eloisa's tiny kitchen. Her food was honest, generous and incredibly delicious, and remains one of my greatest inspirations as a cook.

My Training in the French Kitchen

In 1967 my father retired from the service and we returned to live in Santa Fe. I got my first professional cooking job there in 1971, at a fancy French restaurant that had *haute cuisine* dishes on one side of its menu and tacos, burritos and enchiladas on the other. No one in Santa Fe seemed to think that odd. I cooked the French side, which was much more interesting and "gourmet" to me than the Southwestern food available in any number of local restaurants.

I came to Los Angeles in 1973, and worked in several restaurants there. Cooking in California was just beginning to become more sophisticated and innovative, and on my days off I explored as many new restaurants as possible. In 1975, a gentleman named Jean Bertranou opened a grand-scale French restaurant, named L'Ermitage, that combined the best of the classic kitchen with discreet touches of *nouvelle* cuisine. My first meal there was a revelation, and I still remember it in perfect detail: escargots with smoked ham, chives and a sauce flavored with Chablis; stuffed pigeon with corn cakes; a *feuilleté* of asparagus with *beurre blanc*; and Gâteau L'Ermitage, a flourless chocolate-almond cake. The food tasted so good. I wanted to stand on my chair and applaud the chef.

A year later, though already established as a chef of a small restaurant in Manhattan Beach, I decided that, if I was going to continue to cook, I wanted to hone my skills with the best of teachers. I landed a job at L'Ermitage, and began my apprenticeship under chef-*patron* Jean Bertranou. His kitchen was set up in the classic French fashion: everything was organized to the smallest detail, and ran like clockwork. Every cook had his assigned duty—salads (*garde-manger*), fish (*poissonier*), sauces (*saucier*), pastry (*patissier*), and so on. I was the salad man, but Chef Bertranou allowed me to learn the other stations as well.

Just as the cooking on my great-grandparents' ranch in Abiquiu followed the rhythm of the seasons, so did Bertranou's kitchen have its own complex pattern of cycles. Every single day the pastry chef would replenish the kitchen's supply of ten fresh sorbets; at any given moment, at least one of five different stocks simmered constantly on a stove used for that purpose exclusively. Every week, Michel Blanchet, Bertranou's second in command, prepared five different kinds of terrines, and made a fresh batch of aspic from clarified chicken stock. Every autumn, twenty cases of beautiful gold-and-rose Queen Anne cherries were pickled or brandied and stored in the wine cellar for the coming year.

Bertranou taught me so much more about food and restaurants beyond the cooking skills I acquired at L'Ermitage. He taught me to buy only the best, highest quality ingredients, to be inventive about seeking them out when they weren't readily available, and *never* to settle for second best. His quest for smoked salmon is an excellent example of the standards he set. He wasn't happy buying already smoked salmon, so he went to France to learn how they smoked it there; and, since he used Alaskan salmon at the restaurant, he sent a shipment of it ahead to France so he could perfect his technique on the same type he'd be serving at L'Ermitage. Finally, he purchased a large French smoking machine, photographed it in minute detail, took it apart, shipped it to Los Angeles and then, following his photographs, reassembled it in the L'Ermitage kitchen.

Even more impressive was Bertranou's search for a chicken to match the flavor of the free-range *poulets de Bresse* he had cooked in France. Unable to find any that matched his exacting standards, he and another chef went to southwestern France, Bertranou's homeland, and acquired two dozen fertile chicken eggs. They smuggled them back into the United States, and entered through two different ports so that, if one of them were caught, the other would still have some eggs. Bertranou bought a small farm in Acton, northeast of Los Angeles, and there he raised his exclusive flock of blue-clawed free-range *poulets*.

Jean Bertranou's brilliant restaurant, L'Ermitage was a mere five years old when he died suddenly in 1980. It was a tragic loss, not just of a visionary chef but of a warm generous man. It makes me sad to think that Jean will never come through my kitchen door, never have a meal in my own restaurant.

Saint Estèphe and the Evolution of Modern Southwest Cuisine

While still at L'Ermitage, I started to talk about opening a restaurant with my friend Steve Garcia, another Santa Fe native and a chef in his own right, with whom I had worked in a number of kitchens. We decided to open a *nouvelle* French restaurant in

Manhattan Beach, twenty miles south of Los Angeles. The day we signed the lease on our business, we celebrated with a bottle of 1953 Cos d'Estournel from the Saint-Estèphe region in Bordeaux; Saint Estèphe became the name of our restaurant.

With myself in charge of the kitchen and Steve taking care of finances, wines and the dining-room staff, we opened in October 1980. For the first two years I cooked in the style of the chefs for whom I had worked. But during those years I became aware of the resurgence of interest in American regional cooking. This was beginning to influence even the cooking in French restaurants—especially in California. And at the same time I began to realize how good the cooking of my home in Santa Fe really was.

After one visit home, during the fall of 1982, I returned to Los Angeles with fifteen cases of fresh chimayo chiles. I experimented with the chiles in every course but dessert. They were roasted, pureed and made into sauces; they were diced and put into salad dressings; they were creamed into soups; they were chopped and mixed into poultry stuffings. I loved the way these mild chiles added a slight spark of fire to any dish.

I then set out to develop a separate "menu within a menu" at Saint Estèphe, consisting of a small assortment of French-style appetizers and entrees featuring native New Mexican ingredients. One of the first dishes I created was an hors d'oeuvre of American caviars and smoked salmon, served not on buckwheat blini or toast points but on an authentic bread of the Southwest—blue corn tortillas. The delicate roes and fish had found a perfect counterpoint in the earthiness of the tortillas.

The Southwestern "menu within a menu" made up about 25 percent of all the dishes offered at Saint Estèphe, but within a few short months our guests were ordering 75 percent of their dishes from that menu. I began to create new Southwestern dishes as specials—roasted Anaheim chiles rellenos stuffed with *duxelles*, steamed salmon steaks in sauce decorated with red chile puree and sorrell cream to resemble the painted desert, chocolate "corn on the cob" with mango "kernels." Within the course of the year I had enough specialties to fill a complete menu. In the Spring of 1983, we introduced new menus that read, "Saint Estèphe: Modern Southwest Cuisine."

The Metamorphosis of Traditional Southwestern Dishes into Modern Southwest Cuisine

Wonderful though it is, traditional Southwestern cooking offers a limited palette of basic ingredients—corn, chiles, beans and squashes. For the most part, this has been a common people's cuisine, but, by using a small repertoire of basic preparations, the native Southwestern cook learned to combine and prepare these few ingredients in a wide variety of ways.

In creating dishes for my Modern Southwest Cuisine, I have at my disposal the wide array of ingredients available today. And I can draw not only on my classical training as a chef but also on the cooking styles of all the world's cuisines. A look at my modern variations on traditional Southwestern dishes will help explain my point:

Tamales. Traditional tamales are mixtures of cornmeal flour (*masa*) stuffed with meat, and steamed in a corn husk. As a method of cooking, this differs little from the French concept of cooking food *en papillote* (in paper), or *en plastique* (in plastic wrap). Some of the modern tamales I serve (recipes on pages 66 to 72) are steamed *en plastique* and have a variety of light fillings, however, they also include a layer of *masa* or Spanish rice, and after being unwrapped, are served on a corn husk, which keeps them firmly in touch with their Southwestern origins.

Tacos. Tacos are the sandwiches of the Southwest, soft or fried corn tortillas wrapped around a meat filling with salsa, cheese, lettuce and tomato. I have taken this casual dish and turned it into elegant hors d'oeuvres, filling miniature tortillas with French-style ingredients like truffled scrambled eggs or foie gras (pages 35 to 38). I have also taken the *concept* of tacos as filled edible wrappers and substituted various salad leaves (recipes on pages 81 to 85)—radicchio, Swiss chard, butter lettuce—and stuffed them with anything from shrimp to snails. And I've even created a recipe using a conventional deep-fried taco shell (page 150)—except that the tortilla is made from blue corn, and the taco is filled with duck, artichoke hearts and papaya.

Enchiladas. Most people think of an enchilada as a corn tortilla briefly fried, dipped in chile sauce, rolled around a cheese or meat filling, and baked. But the enchiladas of my childhood were always made with two tortillas—one laid flat on the plate, topped with cheese and onion, smothered with red chile sauce, and topped with the second tortilla. I have adapted this idea of a filling and sauce between two tortillas in my Modern Southwest versions. I cut the tortillas, either blue or gold (or both), into geometric shapes, or I decorate them by branding them with a hot skewer, and I serve them with such innovative fillings as Santa Barbara shrimp with leeks (page 122); escargots with port wines sauce and spinach (page 73) or filet mignon with chanterelles and sorrel sauce (page 161).

Chiles Rellenos. Deep-fried, cheese-stuffed mild chiles seem to accompany every main dish in the traditional Southwest kitchen. I've done away with the heavy batter, the deep-frying and the cheese filling. I stuff my rellenos with the classic French *duxelles* or with fresh cooked lobster (recipes on pages 89 to 91), steam them, and serve them on top of a light sauce. For lavish presentations, I even slice two different colors of chiles rellenos and interchange their pieces to make "zebras" of chiles rellenos (page 92).

Whatever changes and elaborations I make in the development of Modern Southwest Cuisine, I strive to keep the flavors and textures of all my ingredients intact and pure, to let the food speak for itself. I never forget that taste is paramount.

The Look of Modern Southwest Cuisine

As important as taste is to good cooking, a diner's first experience of a meal is visual. So presentation is an essential part of all the Modern Southwest dishes I have developed.

The Southwest offers me a wide variety of visual inspiration. The land itself, with its rich earth tones, is reflected in the colors of cornmeal, in pale-brown pinto bean sauces, in the brick red of dried chiles and the vivid green of cactus. The textures of Southwestern food add another visual dimension: the rough, blistered surfaces of tortillas, the chunky consistency of fresh salsa, the ridged pattern of a dried corn husk etched on a tamale.

An even greater influence comes from native artists of the Southwest. For thousands of years, Southwestern Indian tribes have created objects decorated in both bold and subtle patterns whose strong visual impact remains strikingly contemporary. I have utilized many of these native patterns to decorate my dishes: vegetables arranged like the colorful diamonds of a Navajo blanket, pasta cut in stepped pyramids, sauce essences painted onto plates in the shape of arrows, zigzags and thunderbolts. Many of the photographs in this book contain genuine native artifacts of the Southwest, some of them over a thousand years old.

Though my restaurant and food are modern, I still feel intimately in touch with the old Southwest. For me, the Southwest is an intense spirit—a spirit you can sense in New Mexico's vivid light, its sunbaked deserts, its rugged landscapes and its vital, earthy foods.

I was aware of this spirit only subliminally when my family first came to live in Santa Fe. I took for granted the rich culture of the place—the native artisans as well as the many contemporary artists who settled and exhibited their works there, the annual fiestas and music festivals.

Then, on a crackling-hot summer day in 1971, my mother, Rose, and I stopped by the Ghost Ranch, just outside of Abiquiu, to visit my Aunt Jerry, who worked as cook for the visionary painter Georgia O'Keeffe. While my mother and Jerry talked in the kitchen, I wandered through O'Keeffe's rambling hacienda. The rooms, with their packed dry mud floors and natural log-and-stick ceilings, were lined with the sun-bleached skulls of steers and smaller desert animals. Natural earthenware pots, set in niches and on ledges in the adobe walls, held large collections of rocks separated by size and/or color—brick red, ash grey, bone white, charcoal black. Nature, in the form of five-foot-high sagebrush, ran rampant in the patio at the center of the U-shaped building.

Georgia O'Keeffe and
my aunt Jerry Newson

I passed through a low doorway, just off the patio, into the dining room. And there, at the head of the large, rough wood table, sat Georgia O'Keeffe. She didn't acknowledge my presence; in fact, she probably didn't even know I was there. She stared upward, beyond the ceiling, lost in her own solitary vision.

I left the Ghost Ranch that afternoon filled with a deep sense of my desert homeland stripped to its bare essentials. That intangible feeling of the Southwestern spirit has never left me. Above all else, it is what I try to capture in my cooking.

A Guide to Native Southwestern Ingredients

I utilize many traditional Southwestern foods in Modern Southwest Cuisine. As a rule, you can find them in most well-stocked supermarkets or in ethnic markets. Use the guide below to help you select and prepare these basic ingredients.

Cactus Pears (See Nopales)

Chayote

These pear-shaped, delicately flavored squashes vary in color from creamy white to dark green. They are available from late autumn to spring. Choose firm chayotes. They keep well in the refrigerator for up to 2 weeks.

Chiles

Fresh and dried chiles play an important part in Modern Southwest Cuisine. But I don't try to use every one of the dozens of varieties of chile that are available, though I've tasted and cooked with them all. Instead, I stick to a handful of mild to medium-hot chiles that add subtle spice to recipes without overwhelming them.

FRESH CHILES:

Anaheims. I find dark-green Anaheims among the most pleasant chiles to cook with. They are mildly spicy, slightly sweet and fruity in flavor, and are fairly "fleshy." Their size, 6 to 8 inches long and 1 to 2 inches wide, make them perfect for stuffing. In the late fall, fully ripened red Anaheims are available; these have an even sweeter, somewhat milder flavor than the green.

Chiles del Arbol. These small, shiny, bright red chiles have little flavor, just fire. But they are so attractive that I like to use them as a decorative garnish.

Chimayos. This New Mexican variety of the Anaheim chile has an especially fine, full flavor. I use it whenever possible in the kitchen of Saint Estèphe.

Jalapeños. Though many hotter chiles exist, small dark-green or fully ripened red jalapeños, about 2 inches long and 1 inch wide, are among the hottest of those chiles considered edible by American Southwest standards. I use them not so much for flavoring as for the amount of fire they add to a dish.

Poblanos. These large, tapered chiles, about 5 inches long and up to 3 inches wide, have shiny dark-green skin. Their rich flavor, which may vary from mild to moderately hot, is especially good in sauces for red meats.

Serranos. Smaller, slimmer and somewhat lighter in color than jalapeños, serrano chiles are about the same "temperature" of spiciness. I find, though, that they have a fuller taste when cooked.

STORING FRESH CHILES:

Stored in a cool, dry place, fresh chiles will keep for several weeks. Wrap them loosely in paper towels to absorb moisture and place them in the lower shelf of your refrigerator.

PREPARING FRESH CHILES:

When chiles are used fresh and raw, they are usually seeded first. A chile's flavor comes mostly from its flesh; its seeds are less easy to digest, and are very hot. To seed chiles, simply cut them in half lengthwise and pick or brush out the seeds with your fingertips or the tip of a small sharp knife. Also cut out the white, membranelike ribs or veins inside the chile; they have little flavor, but are the hottest part. Then cut or break off the tough stems.

Roasting intensifies and sweetens the flavor of chiles. To roast chiles, place them over an open flame (either a gas stove or a barbecue grill works fine), or under a hot broiler, and turn them until their skins are evenly blistered and browned; or bake the chiles in a 450°F oven until evenly blackened, about 25 minutes, turning them 2 or 3 times so they roast evenly. When the chiles are cool enough to handle, peel off and discard the skins; pull off the stems and remove the seeds and ribs with a small spoon. Save the juices from inside the chiles: they are very flavorful, and can be added to your dish or other dressings or sauces.

A *word of caution*: The oils of chiles, particularly those from the seeds, are intensely hot. They will cause any small cuts or abrasions on your hands to burn. Wash your hands very thoroughly with soap and water and avoid accidentally touching or rubbing your eyes after working with chiles. Wash all knives, cutting boards and other implements thoroughly before using them for other recipes.

DRIED CHILES AND CHILE POWDERS:

Drying intensifies the heat and flavor of chiles, and most of the larger fresh varieties above are available in dried form. Dried chiles are ground to make chile powders, which vary in heat from mild to hot. The hottest chile powder I use at Saint Estèphe is a *chile pequín*, a coarsely ground powder made from the small dried chiles of the same name.

Store all dried chiles and chile powders in airtight containers in a cool, dry place. They will keep their flavors for up to a year.

Corn

Dried corn, in the form of cornmeal, posole, and tortillas, is the foundation of Southwestern cooking. I love dried corn's earthy, subtly sweet flavor and its robust texture, and use it in its many forms as often as I can in my cooking.

CORNMEAL:

Most people are familiar with the medium-fine gold or yellow cornmeal that is readily available in supermarkets. I prefer to use an old Southwestern staple that is getting so much widespread attention lately that many people regard it as a *new* product: blue cornmeal. Ground from dried kernels of a naturally blue-gray variety of corn, blue cornmeal has a more pronounced flavor than the gold variety, and its muted ashen color can be used to striking effect in recipes.

Store cornmeal in an airtight container in a cool dry place. It will stay fresh for up to a year.

POSOLE:

The hominy of the Southwest, posole is produced by treating the dried kernels of many varieties of corn with lime. Posole is cooked before use in recipes, and it is often eaten as a starchy vegetable alone or with other dishes (page 198).

Store posole in an airtight container in a cool, dry place. If you can't find posole, substitute canned whole hominy.

MASA HARINA AND NIXTAMAL:

Masa harina is a fine gold hominy cornmeal, used to make tamales and corn tortillas.

For tamales, the masa is mixed with other ingredients into a paste known as *nixtamal*. You can buy nixtamal ready-made in Mexican markets. Or you can prepare it yourself using the following recipe:

Nixtamal

TO MAKE ABOUT 1½ CUPS

Stir together the masa, chile powder, salt and baking powder.

With an electric beater, gradually beat about ¼ of the masa mixture into the lard. Then gradually beat in about 2 tablespoons of the water. Continue alternately beating in the masa and water until they are fully incorporated; then beat the mixture until smooth and light, about 3 minutes longer. Store nixtamal in the refrigerator.

1 cup masa harina
1 teaspoon mild chile powder
½ teaspoon salt
⅛ teaspoon baking powder
¼ cup lard, softened
½ cup lukewarm water

TORTILLAS:

Tortillas are the bread of the Southwest. Corn tortillas are sold in a number of different sizes and thicknesses; in my cooking, and in the recipes in this book, I use a thin, medium-size 6-to-7 inch tortilla. Buy one of the good-quality commercial varieties, and store them in the refrigerator, sealed in plastic wrap, for up to a week.

Jícama

The thick brown skin and lumpy shape of this tuberous vegetable conceal a crisp, white, slightly sweet flesh that makes jícama an excellent vegetable for salads or side dishes. Be sure to peel it thickly to remove the fibrous layer that lies just beneath the skin.

Choose firm roots with a minimum of blemishes. Uncut, Jícama will keep in the refrigerator for up to 2 weeks.

Nopales (Cactus Pears)

The succulent, flat pads of the nopal cactus are eaten as a vegetable or in salads in the Southwest. Their fruit, known as tuna or cactus pear, has a rich, tart, raspberry-red flesh that I find refreshing. Both the fruit and the pads are available fresh in Mexican markets. The pads should be deep green; the fruit should be green ripening to rosy-red. The pads can also be purchased, cut up, in cans.

Handle fresh nopal pads carefully to avoid catching the spines in your skin; hold them with a thick kitchen towel while you pare off the small tufts of spines and the tough edge of the pad with a small, sharp knife or a vegetable peeler.

Pine Nuts

Known in the Southwest as *piñones*, these plump, rice-shaped seeds come from the large cones of pines that grow throughout New Mexico. Their flavor is fully developed by toasting: spread them on a baking tray and leave them in a preheated 425°F oven until golden, 5 to 10 minutes, turning them several times to keep them from scorching. In Italian and other ethnic markets they may be sold as *pignoli*.

Pumpkin Seeds

Shelled pumpkins seeds are used whole as a snack or a garnish in the Southwest; ground, they frequently serve as a thickener for sauces. To roast them for a fuller flavor, spread the seeds on a baking tray and bake them in a preheated 425°F oven until golden, 5 to 10 minutes, turning them several times to keep them from scorching.

Tomatillos

Sometimes referred to as green tomatoes, tomatillos are actually relatives of the tomato; they remain green when ripe, and resemble small green tomatoes encased in dry brown husks. They have a mild, slightly tart flavor, and are excellent in salads, sauces and soups.

A Word on Wines with Modern Southwest Cuisine

My partner at Saint Estèphe, Steve Garcia, personally selects the list of more than 150 wines to accompany our menu. Here, Steve offers his own thoughts on choosing wines to serve with Modern Southwest Cuisine.

"Some wine experts throw their hands up in horror at the thought of serving fine wines with highly spiced cooking. When they first hear of Modern Southwest Cuisine, they may have that same reaction, thinking our food is fiery hot with chiles.

"But at Saint Estèphe, chiles play a very subtle role in a highly refined cuisine. So I follow the same rules anyone should when matching wines and food. Just as a well-planned menu progresses from light, simple foods to more complex, filling dishes, and then on to dessert, so should your choice of wines to serve with the recipes in this book follow a logical progression.

"I keep this simple logic in mind when planning the wine list at Saint Estèphe. And, since we are in California, I take good advantage of the outstanding offerings of the state's wineries.

"Our wine list begins with California sauvignon blancs, which make an excellent start to a meal. They are light in taste, lower in alcohol, than the heavier chardonnays, and have a unique softness. I seek out dry sauvignons reminiscent of the classic French Chablis. Some of my favorites are the sauvignon blancs of Cakebread Cellars and the superb fumé blancs made by Robert Mondavi. Such wines make perfect companions to our hors d'oeuvres of Blue Corn Tortillas with Smoked Salmon and Two Types of American Caviar (page 35), or any of our appetizer tamales (pages 66 to 72).

"Next come chardonnays, some of the most phenomenal wines produced in California. You can find many different styles of the wine, variously described as buttery, apple-y, oaky, and so on. I prefer chardonnays on the dry side, with just a touch of fruit. Those of Long Vineyards in the Napa Valley are in the traditional Burgundian style, very clean and crisp; they would be perfect with any of our seafood entrees, especially the salmon dishes (pages 127 to 130). And I'm very excited by the chardonnays produced at Ventana, in Monterey, by Doug Meader, one of the finest winemakers I know. He experiments, breaking new ground, as we try to do at Saint Estèphe. His rich, oaky wine goes beautifully with a poultry dish like Breast of Chicken with Jícama (page 142), one of the favorite entrees on our menu.

"The cabernet sauvignons of California are suberb wines, comparable, I think, to the reds of Bordeaux. The cabernet made by William Hill in Napa has a finesse and balance that approaches the best of France, and would be ideal with a full-flavored meat entree such as Veal Chops Marinated in Burnt Chile Pesto (page 156). Mondavi's offering has a dry, clear, slightly earthy finish that goes beautifully with Duck with Posole (page 148). Heitz Cellar's cabernets have a crisp, almost minty quality—perfect for a number of meat or chicken dishes.

"Soft, velvety zinfandels, distinctively fruity, yet dry, are among the most typical wines of California. I pour a wine such as the one produced at Lytton Springs, in Sonoma, with a light, meaty entree—the veal chop or the Breast of Chicken with Passionfruit Butter (page 141). A big zinfandel such as Cakebread's is bold enough to serve with an entree as rich as Enchilada of Filet Mignon (page 161).

"Which leads us to dessert and the end of the meal. I like to finish a meal with a glass of one of California's world-class sparkling wines. Among my favorites are those of Domaine Chandon, Schramsberg, Iron Horse and Ventana. Any would go nicely with a light fruit dessert such as the Neon Tumbleweed (page 192). The Tumbleweed is also nicely accompanied by one of California's nectarlike late-harvest Rieslings—particularly those produced by Joseph Phelps and Château St. Jean. Sometimes I like a small glass of this sublime wine on its own for dessert.

"I couldn't complete this brief discussion without mentioning the young wine industry of our home state, New Mexico. When I was growing up, wineries just outside of Santa Fe, near Dixon, made simple table wines, without much distinction. With our high elevations and harsh winter temperatures, this was always a hard area for grape cultivation. But now a few wineries are beginning to take advantage of new discoveries in the science of winemaking to overcome nature, and I've been impressed by such wines as the excellent local Riesling made by a winery called La Chiripada—a name that means "Stroke of Luck."

"The most exciting advances in New Mexican wine, though, are happening in the southern part of the state. There, a number of new boutique-style wineries are making the most of a climate and elevation that approach those of Bordeaux, with warm summers and cool, but not freezing, winters. One of these young, adventurous vineyards, St. Clair, is the first New Mexican winery to be represented on the list at Saint Estèphe—by a sauvignon blanc that compares favorably with the best of California's, and a very light, fruity and slightly sweet dessert wine made from muscat canelli grapes, the same grapes used in Italian Asti Spumante. As our homeland's wine industry continues to grow and develop, I look forward to serving more New Mexican wines with the Modern Southwest Cuisine of Saint Estèphe."

A Note on Presentation for the Home Cook

Throughout this book, the photographs show my food exactly as I present it to guests at Saint Estèphe. And the recipes give you detailed instructions on how to duplicate my presentation style.

Do not feel, however, that you must serve the recipes to your own guests in precisely the same style. If you like, try duplicating my dishes as I present them, and tell your guests that the food they are eating looks just like it does in the restaurant. But if your serving platters or dinner service are a different size, shape or color, or if you have some trouble mastering one of my presentation techniques, don't let it bother you. Adapt the recipe's presentation to suit your own style and your own time and abilities.

Remember that it is the food's taste that is most important. Above all else, I want you to have fun preparing, serving and eating the foods in my recipes.

CHAPTER 1

HORS D'OEUVRES

Rattlesnake of Smoked Salmon

A food illustrator I know once loaned me a copy of an out-of-print Southwestern cookbook called *Rattlesnake Under Glass*. I began to toy with the idea of doing a recipe using rattlesnake, which some people consider a delicacy.

Frankly, I haven't come up with a rattlesnake recipe yet—at least not one I'd serve at Saint Estèphe. But I have devised an hors d'oeuvre that uses this indigenous reptile as a motif for a colorful presentation of smoked salmon.

TO SERVE 6

1 small red bell pepper, roasted, peeled and seeded (page 22)
6 hard-boiled egg yolks, finely chopped
4 ounces smoked salmon, finely chopped
1 bunch parsley, stemmed, leaves finely chopped
1 medium onion, finely chopped
6 tablespoons capers, drained
Gorditas (page 196)

Cut a thin, tapered triangle about 1 inch long from the pepper for the snake's tail; cut 2 small triangles for the eyes, and a long forked shape for the tongue. Reserve the rest of the pepper for another recipe.

Place the tail at one side of a large serving platter. From the tail, arrange a tapered ½-inch-long section of egg yolk, widening to about 1 inch. Then alternate sections of capers, salmon, onion, parsley and egg yolk, winding across the platter like a snake. At the other end of the platter, attached to the body, shape a snake's head of egg yolk and decorate it with a red pepper eyes and tongue.

Serve the "rattlesnake" with Gorditas.

Terrine of Arizona Shrimp with Corn and Green Chiles

Believe it or not, shrimp are being raised in the Arizona desert. Giant Malaysian freshwater prawns, once served only to Asian royalty, are now being commercially bred in geothermally warmed lakes on farms near Yuma. We use these large, plump, sweet shrimp—which weigh over 1½ ounces each—in a terrine we serve as an appetizer at Saint Estèphe. If your local fish shop can't get them for you, use any large fresh shrimp.

Rattlesnake of Smoked Salmon

TO SERVE 6

1½ pounds Arizona shrimp (or other large shrimp), peeled and deveined, tails removed, patted dry
2 cups heavy cream
½ teaspoon salt
½ teaspoon white pepper
1 egg
4 large green Anaheim chiles, roasted, peeled, stemmed and seeded (page 22) and coarsely chopped
1 cup cooked corn kernels
Gorditas (page 196) or toast points
Red Chile Pesto (page 206)
Gold Corn Preserves (page 206)

Preheat the oven to 350°F. Put the shrimp, cream, salt and pepper in a food processor and process until smoothly pureed. Add the egg and pulse until it is blended in. Remove the puree from the processor bowl and fold in the chiles and the corn.

Butter a 2-quart loaf pan and spoon the puree into it, smoothing its surface. Cut a piece of waxed paper or parchment paper just big enough to fit inside the pan, and place it on top of the shrimp mixture. Place the pan inside a larger baking dish. Place the baking dish on the oven shelf and carefully pour enough boiling water into it to come halfway up the sides of the loaf pan.

Bake the terrine until firm, about 45 minutes. Let the terrine cool to room temperature. Peel off the paper, unmold the terrine and cut into ½-inch thick slices; cut the slices into 1-inch squares. Serve the terrine with Gorditas or toast points, Red Chile Pesto and Gold Corn Preserves.

Kachina Mosaic of Caviars with Endive Feathers

Kachinas are the spirit messengers of the Pueblo Indians, protecting them, carrying their prayers to the gods and bringing rain. *Kachina dolls* are favorite children's toys, and during religious festivals native dancers wear brightly painted Kachina masks. The dolls and masks are favorites with collectors of native American art.

This arrangement of caviars, chopped eggs and onions gets its pattern from the faces of Kachina dolls and Kachina masks. It's surprising how closely its colors match the vivid paints actually used by the Indians in their folk art.

Kachina Mosaic of Caviars with Endive Feathers

TO SERVE 4

1 pound large Belgian endives,
    leaves separated
2 hard-boiled eggs
3 tablespoons American golden
    caviar (whitefish roe)
2 tablespoons finely chopped
    fresh parsley
3 tablespoons American sturgeon
    caviar
1 tablespoon salmon caviar
1 tablespoon finely chopped
    onion

Select about 2 dozen of the best endive leaves of roughly equal size (about 5 inches long). Set them aside.

Separate the yolks from the whites of the eggs. Finely chop both.

Draw a circle 7 inches in diameter on a sheet of paper. Following the photograph on the previous page, or your own imagination, draw a Kachina doll face in the circle. Place a 7-inch glass plate on top of the circle and use the circle and the doll face as your guide to assembling the Kachina doll mosaic. Center the plate with the completed mosaic on top of a 12-inch serving plate; place a rim of endive leaves completely surrounding and radiating from the mosaic like a feather headdress.

Peppered Oysters

I created this hors d'oeuvre as part of the opening night buffet for the Maya exhibition at the Los Angeles County Natural History Museum. Use only absolutely fresh oysters. I prefer imported French Belons or Malpeques from Prince Edward Island in Canada. The red chile sauce accentuates the fresh ocean flavor of the oysters.

TO SERVE 6

24 oysters, shucked, 1 cup of
    their liquid reserved
    (supplemented, if necessary,
    with bottled clam juice)
 4 dried ancho chiles, wiped
    clean with a dry cloth, soaked
    in warm water until soft,
    stemmed and seeded
    (page 22)
¼ cup lime juice
 6 garlic cloves
 2 tablespoons olive oil
 2 teaspoons whole white
    peppercorns, crushed
½ teaspoon salt
 3 limes, quartered

Put the oyster liquid, 2 chiles, the lime juice, garlic, oil, peppercorns and salt into a food processor. Process until smoothly pureed. Remove from processor. Finely chop the remaining 2 chiles and stir them into the sauce.

Place the shucked oysters in their half-shells on a bed of crushed ice. Spoon the sauce on top. Serve with lime wedges.

Blue Corn Tortillas with Smoked Salmon and Two Types of American Caviar

I think of these as open-faced caviar and smoked salmon mini-enchiladas. And I really like the playful contradictions they offer: the combination of two worlds, the domestic and the aristocratic, the rough tortillas topped with their ultra-elite accompaniments. Best of all, the simple but hearty corn flavor is a great foil for the elegant and rich fish roes.

TO SERVE 6

Preheat the oven to 350°F.

With a cookie cutter, cut each tortilla into 3 1-inch circles or triangles (the job goes more quickly if you stack them 2 or 3 at a time). Wrap the cut-out tortillas in a sheet of buttered aluminum foil. Bake in the oven for only 2 minutes—just until they're warm and tender; do not overcook them. Remove the tortillas from the foil and pat them with paper towels to remove excess butter.

Top each tortilla with ½ teaspoon of sour cream and ¼ teaspoon of chopped onion. Top 6 each of the little tortillas or triangles with 1 teaspoon of golden caviar, 1 teaspoon of sturgeon caviar and a ½-inch piece of smoked salmon. Garnish each with a sprig of dill, and place a few capers on each salmon tortilla.

With a narrow spatula, transfer the tortillas to a warmed serving platter. Serve immediately.

6 large blue (or gold) corn tortillas
1 tablespoon unsalted butter
3 tablespoons sour cream
1½ tablespoons finely chopped red onion
3 tablespoons American golden caviar (whitefish roe)
3 tablespoons American sturgeon caviar
4½ ounces smoked salmon, sliced
Fresh dill sprigs, for garnish
1 tablespoon capers, for garnish

Blue Corn Tacos with Oeufs Truffes

Oeufs truffes—creamy eggs lightly scrambled with slivered black truffle—is one of the most luxuriously rich yet simple dishes in French cuisine. I find these eggs make an excellent and beautiful filling for miniature blue corn tacos. There's no need to go out and buy a whole truffle for this dish; canned truffle shavings, a slightly more economical luxury, are fine.

2 large blue corn tortillas
1 tablespoon unsalted butter
2 eggs, beaten
2 tablespoons half-and-half
½ teaspoon salt
½ teaspoon white pepper
1½ ounce black truffle, cut into small slivers, or same amount of drained canned truffle shavings

Stack the 2 tortillas and cut 3 circles from each with a 2½-inch cookie cutter or inverted glass. Wrap the 6 circles of tortilla in a sheet of waxed paper, folding and pleating the paper to seal them in.

Bring water to a boil in a steamer or a saucepan with a steaming rack. Steam the wrapped tortillas for about 2 minutes, until tender.

While the tortillas are steaming, melt the butter in a small saucepan over moderate heat. Add the eggs, half and half, salt and pepper and cook, whisking continuously, until smooth, thick and creamy, about 1 minute. Stir in the truffles.

Remove the tortillas from the steamer, unwrap them and pat them dry with a paper towel. Spoon the scrambled egg into the tortillas and fold them over into a taco shape. Serve immediately.

Gold Corn Tacos with Foie Gras and Gold Corn Preserves

The earthy flavor of the tortillas and the intense richness of foie gras—the buttery liver of specifically raised geese—make a wonderful contrast. A relish made from fresh sweet corn plays the same role as salsa does in more conventional tacos.

Fresh raw foie gras is cooked only very briefly, sliced ¼-inch thick and sautéed in butter. If you like, use canned foie gras for these tacos. Available from gourmet stores, it is an excellent product, already cooked, with a taste as rich and flavorful as fresh. You might also want to try using the domestic fresh foie gras now being produced in the United States.

2 gold corn tortillas
4½ ounces foie gras, fresh or canned (see above)
1 tablespoon Gold Corn Preserves (page 206)

Stack the 2 tortillas and cut 3 circles from each with a 2½-inch cookie cutter or inverted glass. Wrap the 6 circles of tortilla in a sheet of waxed paper, folding and pleating the paper to seal them in.

Top: Gold Corn Tacos with Foie Gras and Gold Corn Preserves, and Layer Cake of Blue and Gold Corn Tortillas. Bottom: Blue Corn Tacos with Oeufs Truffes, and Blue Corn Tortillas with Smoked Salmon and Two Types of American Caviar

Bring water to a boil in a steamer or a saucepan with a steaming rack. Steam the wrapped tortillas for about 2 minutes, until soft.

Unwrap the tortillas and pat them dry with a paper towel.

Spoon about ½ teaspoon of foie gras onto each. Gently fold the tortillas in half around foie gras, forming a taco shape. Spoon about ½ teaspoon of Gold Corn Preserves into each taco. Pass them from an hors d'oeuvre platter.

Layer Cake of Blue and Gold Corn Tortillas

I've always liked the look of *bagatelles*, the classic French pastries made up of pastel-colored layers of génoise cake, marzipan, buttercream and fruit. They gave me the idea for these savory bite-sized hors d'oeuvres with layers of tortilla in 2 colors, goat cheese, spinach and smoked salmon.

TO MAKE 6 PIECES

1 bunch spinach, washed and stemmed
4 ounces aged creamy goat cheese, such as Montrachet
1 tablespoon finely chopped onion
½ teaspoon salt
½ teaspoon white pepper
3 7-inch blue corn tortillas
3 7-inch gold corn tortillas
Vegetable oil for deep frying
2 ounces smoked salmon, thinly sliced

Bring 2 quarts of water with 1 teaspoon of salt to a rolling boil in a large saucepan. Plunge the spinach into the water, then immediately drain it and let it cool. With your hands, squeeze out all the excess water from the spinach. Put the spinach in a processor and puree it for about 1 minute. Set aside.

In a small bowl, mash the goat cheese together with the onion, salt and pepper, until well mixed. Set it aside.

Stack the tortillas and cut each into a 2¾-by-3½-inch rectangle. In a heavy skillet, heat ½ inch of oil to a temperature of 375°F. on a deep-frying thermometer. Fry the tortillas for about 30 seconds, until tender, soft and flexible. Pat them dry with paper towels. Do not overcrowd the skillet—fry in batches if necessary.

Place ⅓ of the cheese mixture on top of a gold corn tortilla rectangle, spreading the cheese evenly right to the edges of the tortilla. Place a blue tortilla on top and spread it with all of the spinach puree, right up to the edges. Place a gold tortilla on top and spread it with another ⅓ of the cheese. Top it with another blue tortilla and arrange the sliced salmon on top of that. Finish the layering with a final gold tortilla, the rest of the cheese, and a final blue tortilla. Pat the "layer cake" gently to compress the layers.

Wrap the cake in plastic wrap and put it in the freezer for about 45 minutes, until firm enough to slice. Unwrap and, with a sharp knife, trim about ¼ inch from each edge, wiping the knife after each cut, to give the sides neatly defined layers. Then cut the rectangular cake in half lengthwise and, wiping the knife after each cut, slice each half into 3 equal pieces. Serve chilled.

Duck Liver Mousse
with Bouquet of Pickled Chiles in Aspic

An abundance of pickled Southwestern chiles, prepared 2 days in advance, make a striking and piquant garnish for this classic French provincial hors d'oeuvre.

TO SERVE 6

For the Pickled Chiles: Put the vinegar, garlic, shallot, salt and pepper in a large saucepan and bring them to a boil over high heat. Wash the chiles and put them in a jar; pour the boiling vinegar mixture over them. Let the jar cool to room temperature, cover it and leave the chiles to marinate at cool room temperature for 2 days.

For the Duck Liver Mousse: Preheat the oven to 325°F. Put the livers in a processor and pulse a few times to chop the livers coarsely. With the motor running, gradually add the cream, brandy and seasonongs, until the mixture is smooth.

Press the mousse mixture through a fine sieve, and transfer it to a 1-quart oval terrine or baking dish, smoothing its surface. Cut a piece of waxed paper or parchment paper just big enough to fit inside the terrine and place it on top of the mousse mixture. Place the terrine inside a larger pan or baking dish. Place the pan on the oven shelf and carefully pour enough boiling water into the pan to come halfway up the sides of the terrine.

Bake the mousse for 45 minutes. Take it from the oven, remove it carefully from the pan of water, and let it cool to room temperature—about 1½ hours.

◤▱ *Pickled Chiles*
  1 quart white wine vinegar
  1 whole garlic clove, peeled
  1 whole shallot, peeled
  1 tablespoon salt
  1 tablespoon pepper
  3 fresh green jalapeño chiles
  3 fresh yellow jalapeño chiles
  3 fresh green serrano chiles
  3 fresh red serrano chiles
  2 long green Anaheim chiles

◤▱ *Duck Liver Mousse*
  1 pound duck livers (or chicken livers), carefully trimmed of all membranes and veins
1½ cups heavy cream
  5 tablespoons brandy
  ½ teaspoon salt
  ½ teaspoon white pepper

continued

For the Aspic: Put the consommé in a small saucepan and boil it until it has reduced to 1 cup, about 15 minutes. Stir the gelatin powder into the hot consommé and let it cool until steam no longer rises from its surface.

Meanwhile, carefully peel the paper from the surface of the mousse. Take the chiles out of their marinade and pat them dry with paper towels. Cut each chile in half lengthwise. Arrange the chiles as decorations, cut sides down, on top of the mousse in a bouquet design.

Pour the aspic into the terrine, covering the mousse and the chiles. Chill the mousse in the refrigerator for at least 3 hours. Serve with toast points.

◤◢ *Aspic*
2 cups Basic Consommé
   (page 48)
2 teaspoons unflavored gelatin
   powder

Corncob of Queso Blanco with Condiments from the Southwest Pantry

A seasoned fresh cream cheese, sculpted into the shape of a large corn cob, makes a very attractive hors d'oeuvre for a buffet table. Surround the cob with an assortment of condiments from the Southwest Pantry (Chapter 9) such as Jalapeño Preserves, Gold Corn Preserves, Red Chile Pesto, Grandma Eloisa's Apricot Preserves, Pineapple-Cilantro Salsa and Pickled Chiles, along with crisp blue and gold tortilla chips and miniature Gorditas (see recipes starting on page 196).

Fresh, soft, moldable cream cheese, *queso blanco*, can be found in most Mexican markets. If unavailable, a commercial variety of cream cheese is an acceptable substitute.

If you like, decorate the wide end of the cheese cob with strips of dried corn husk, to look as if they have just been peeled back from the ear of corn.

Duck Liver Mousse with Bouquet of Pickled Chiles in Aspic

3 pounds queso blanco (or other commercial cream cheese)
½ small onion, finely chopped
1 large garlic clove, finely chopped
1 teaspoon white pepper
4 dried corn husks, torn into 1-inch-wide strips, for garnish (available in Latin markets—or use husks from fresh ears)

Divide the cheese into several pieces and put them in a processor with the onion, garlic and pepper. Process until everything is smoothly blended, stopping to scrape down the bowl several times.

Remove the cheese from the processor bowl to a serving platter, and shape it into a cylinder tapered at one end. Chill the cheese in the refrigerator for at least 2 hours.

With the rounded tip of a blunt knife, carve parallel lines about ½ inch deep and ½ inch apart along the length of the cylinder; then carve another set of parallel lines across the cylinder, perpendicular to the first set, to make a grid on the surface of the cheese. Then, with the tip of the knife, sculpt each square of the grid into a rounded corn kernel shape, reserving the bits of cheese left from the carving for another recipe.

Decorate the wide end of the cheese cob with the strips of corn husk. Serve the cob surrounded by bowls filled with Southwestern condiments, chips and tortillas.

Santa Fe Roll with Avocado Vinaigrette

One of the most popular sushi variations of the eighties seems to be the "California Roll," a wrapper of nori seaweed surrounding sushi rice, shrimp or crab, and—the ingredient that defines the preparation—avocado.

The shape of the California Roll was my starting point for this appetizer, featuring native Southwestern ingredients. The wrapper is a flour tortilla. Inside, cooked black beans replace the rice, accompanied by pureed spinach and strips of roasted bell pepper. In place of shrimp or crab, I like the way smoked fish combines with the heartiness of the beans; I usually use smoked sturgeon or, when available, smoked Hawaiian wahoo (a flavorful variety of mackerel). As a nod to the recipe's California-Japanese origins, I serve the Santa Fe Roll with an Avocado Vinaigrette, which is a light, creamy guacamole sauce.

Use a very sharp knife for slicing the roll, to avoid squashing its shape as

Corncob of Queso Blanco with Condiments from the Southwest Pantry

you cut it. If you have trouble cutting through the tortilla, it helps if you nick the top of the roll with the knife tip before each slice.

TO SERVE 6

◄▫ Avocado Vinaigrette
¼ cup walnut oil
4 tablespoons red wine vinegar
1 teaspoon salt
1 teaspoon black pepper
¼ cup sour cream
1 ripe avocado, peeled, seeded and cut into 1-inch chunks

◄▫ Santa Fe Roll
1 cup dried black beans, rinsed
4 cups water
2 medium garlic cloves, finely chopped
1 ounce salt pork, finely diced
1 teaspoon salt
2 bunches spinach, washed and stemmed
2 quarts water
1 teaspoon salt
1 extra large (12-inch) flour tortilla
2 ounces smoked sturgeon, sliced ¼ inch thick
2 red bell peppers, roasted, peeled and seeded (page 22) and cut into ¼-inch-thick strips

For the Avocado Vinaigrette: Put the oil, vinegar, salt and pepper in a processor and pulse to blend them. Pulse in the sour cream, then the avocado to make a light, creamy puree. Put the dressing in the refrigerator to chill.

For the Santa Fe Roll: Put the beans in a medium saucepan with the 4 cups of water, the garlic, salt pork and 1 teaspoon salt. Bring the water to a boil, then reduce the heat and simmer the beans 1½ to 2 hours, until they are tender. Drain the beans and put them in a processor. Pulse until the beans are coarsely pureed. Set them aside.

Bring 2 quarts of water to a rolling boil with 1 teaspoon of salt in a large saucepan. Plunge the spinach into the water, then immediately drain it and let it cool. With your hands, squeeze out all excess water from the spinach. Put the spinach in a processor and puree it, about 1 minute.

Briefly cook the tortilla over a medium-hot grill or under a broiler, about 10 seconds per side. Place the tortilla on the work surface and spread a ¼-inch-thick and 3-inch-wide horizontal row of the beans across its center, ending about 1 inch from either side of the tortilla. Above the beans, spread a ⅛-inch-thick and 1-inch-wide row of spinach puree; above the spinach, a ½-inch wide row of sturgeon; above the sturgeon, another 1-inch-wide row of spinach. Below the central row of beans, place another ½-inch wide row of sturgeon; below that, a 1-inch-wide row of pepper strips; then a final 1-inch-wide row of beans.

With a sharp knife, trim off about 1 inch from the bottom flap of the tortilla. Then, from the bottom, roll up the tortilla, compacting it and smoothing its shape with your hands as you roll it. Cut off the rough ends of the roll, about 1 inch from each side. Then, wiping the knife blade after each slice, cut the roll into 18 rounds, each about ½ inch thick.

Spoon the Avocado Vinaigrette into the middle of each chilled serving plate. Place 3 discs of Santa Fe Roll on top, in a triangular arrangement.

Santa Fe Roll with Avocado Vinaigrette and New Mexican Sushi with New England Lobster

New Mexican Sushi with New England Lobster

Many different varieties of Japanese sushi are made by rolling up seasoned sticky sushi rice with seafood or vegetables in a sheet of dried *nori* seaweed. This is my own Southwestern version of the nori roll, filled with spicy Spanish rice and strips of boiled New England lobster.

Instead of using your regular work surface to prepare the sushi, you might find it easier to do this on top of the small bamboo mat especially made for rolling up the filled sheets of nori; these mats are available at Japanese markets and some gourmet stores. If you don't have the bamboo roller, make this right on your work surface, taking care to do it slowly and using your hands to keep the roll even and compact.

TO SERVE 6

½ cup short-grain glutinous rice, rinsed
1 tomato, peeled, seeded and cut into ½-inch cubes
1 fresh jalapeño chile, stemmed, seeded and finely chopped
1 garlic clove, finely chopped
½ green bell pepper, stemmed, seeded and cut into ½-inch dice
½ small onion, finely chopped
¼ cup cooked corn kernels
1 teaspoon salt
½ teaspoon black pepper
A 1½-pound lobster, boiled for 10 minutes and cooled
3 7-by-8-inch sheets nori

Put the rice, tomato, chile, garlic, pepper, onion, corn and seasonings in a small saucepan. Add enough cold water to cover them by about ½ inch. Bring to a boil over moderate heat, stir once, then cover the pan, reduce the heat, and simmer until all the liquid has been absorbed, 15 to 20 minutes. Remove the pan from the heat and let the rice sit, covered, for about 10 minutes. Stir briefly with a two-pronged fork, cover again and let it sit for 10 minutes more. Then uncover the pan and let the rice cool to room temperature.

While the rice cools, shell the lobster, removing all the meat from the tail and claws. Cut the meat into long strips about ½ inch wide.

Place a sheet of nori on the work surface, shiny side up with a long edge near you. Brush the sheet very lightly with water. Spread about 6 tablespoons of rice in a rectangle about 3 inches wide and 8 inches long, about 1 inch from the edge nearest you. Place a row of lobster meat along the far edge of the rice. Roll up the sheet of seaweed, compacting it with your hands. Then use a sharp knife to cut the sheet into 8 pieces (many nori sheets have slight perforations to show you where to cut). Repeat with the remaining 2 sheets.

CHAPTER 2

SOUPS

Basic Consommé

I use this rich chicken broth as the basis for a wide variety of soups. The mixture of egg whites and aromatic vegetables, stirred into the broth and then skimmed out, removes all impurities from the liquid, giving it the crystal clarity that is the hallmark of a consommé.

TO MAKE ABOUT 9 CUPS

The Consommé
1 whole 2½-pound chicken
3 medium carrots, cut into 1-inch chunks
3 celery stalks, cut into 1-inch chunks
1 large leek, halved lengthwise, washed thoroughly and cut into 1-inch pieces
3 bay leaves
1 bunch parsley
1 teaspoon thyme
5 quarts water

For Clarification
3 egg whites, lightly beaten
1 onion, cut into ¼-inch dice
1 carrot, cut into ¼-inch dice
1 celery stalk, cut into ¼-inch dice

For the Consommé: Put the chicken, carrots, celery, leek, bay leaves, parsley, thyme and water in a large stockpot. Bring them to a boil over moderate heat, skimming frequently to remove all foam from the surface as it rises. When no more foam rises, adjust the heat to maintain a brisk simmer and continue cooking, uncovered, for about 2½ hours, until the liquid has reduced by about half.

To Clarify the Consommé: Sieve the consommé, removing all the solids; reserve the chicken for a salad or some other use. Put the consommé in a medium saucepan over moderate heat and when it comes to a boil, adjust the heat to maintain the barest simmer. Stir together the egg whites and diced vegetables. Pour them quickly into the consommé, stir once, then skim them out as the cooked egg white and vegetables rise to the surface, carrying all impurities with them.

Zuni Consommé Printanière

No soup is lighter, more delicate than a consommé—literally the consummate broth, simmered for hours and cleansed to a beautiful amber clarity. Such a soup requires only the simplest of garnishes, and the French often add just barely cooked springtime vegetables, *à la printanière*. I like to prepare my vegetable garnishes for consommé in a geometric Indian-style pattern arranged in shallow soup bowls that come to the table accompanied by cassolettes or pitchers of soup. The plate decoration is completed with an arrow of Green Sorrel Indian Paint and a few stripes of Red Chile Indian Paint, which dissolve when the soup is added, to give the classic French-style consommé a touch of Southwestern fire.

TO SERVE 6

For the Consommé: Put the chicken, carrots, celery, leek, bay leaves, parsley, thyme and water in a large stockpot. Bring them to a boil over moderate heat, skimming frequently to remove all foam as it rises from the surface. When no more foam rises, adjust the heat to maintain a gentle simmer and continue cooking, uncovered, for about 2½ hours, until the liquid has reduced by about half.

   To Clarify the Consommé: Sieve the consommé, removing all the solids. (Save the chicken for some other use.) Put the consommé in a medium saucepan over moderate heat and when it comes to a boil, adjust the heat to maintain the barest simmer. Stir together the egg whites and diced vegetables. Pour them quickly into the consommé, stir once, then skim them out as the cooked egg white and vegetables rise to the surface, carrying all impurities in the broth with them. Set the consommé aside.

   For the Printanière Garnish: Trim the turnip, carrot and beet into long 4-sided wedges, with sides 1 inch long, which in cross-section have a diamond shape. Cut each wedge crosswise into thin slices, ⅛ to ¼ inch thick, to make a total of 24 diamonds of turnip and 18 each of carrot and beet.
   Bring 2 quarts of water to a boil in a large saucepan with 2 teaspoons of kosher salt. Blanch the vegetable diamonds in the boiling water in separate batches, removing each with a slotted spoon or wire skimmer (or use a basket) and draining it separately on paper towels: blanch first the turnips for 45 seconds,

The Consommé

1 whole 2½-pound chicken
3 medium carrots, cut into 1-inch chunks
3 celery stalks, cut into 1-inch chunks
1 large leek, halved lengthwise, washed thoroughly and cut into 1-inch pieces
3 bay leaves
1 bunch parsley
1 teaspoon thyme
5 quarts water

For Clarification

3 egg whites, lightly beaten
1 onion, diced ¼ inch
1 carrot, diced ¼ inch
1 celery stalk, diced ¼ inch

Printanière Garnish

1 large raw turnip, peeled
1 medium raw carrot, peeled
1 medium raw beet, peeled
2 teaspoons kosher salt
3 ounces Green Sorrel Indian Paint (page 210)
3 ounces Red Chile Indian Paint (page 209)

Zuni Consommé Printanière

then the carrots for 1 minute and, last, the beets for 2½ minutes. Pat each batch of vegetables thoroughly dry.

Place a row of 4 turnip diamonds side by side across the center of each shallow heated soup plate. Place a row of 3 carrot diamonds interlocking below the row of turnips, and a row of 3 beet diamonds interlocking above.

Put the Indian Paints in separate small squeeze bottles. With the Green Sorrel Indian Paint, draw a crooked arrow above each row of beet diamonds, with arrowhead at one end and feather lines at the other. With the Red Chile Indian Paint, paint a pair of parallel zigzag lines below each row of carrot diamonds, following their shapes; add 2 dots below the lines.

Heat the consommé in its saucepan over moderate heat until it comes to a boil. Transfer to a heated tureen or to individual heated serving pitchers. Place a garnished soup plate in front of each guest, accompanied by the consommé to be served at table.

Consommé with Transparent Ravioli of Fresh Herbs and Slivered Chile Garnish

This recipe was inspired by a specialty of the great Milanese chef Gualtiero Marchesi, pioneer of Italy's *nuova cucina*. In my version, I include a favorite Southwestern herb, cilantro. And I add a garnish of slivered dried Chimayo chiles—which add a touch of color and fire to the broth, but are *not* meant to be actually eaten.

Use fresh egg pasta dough for the ravioli. Roll it as thinly as you can with your pasta machine, then roll it out even thinner by hand so it will be translucent when cooked. If you like, you can substitute 36 small Chinese wonton skins, available in most supermarkets, for the pasta; I find them to be of excellent quality, and they make good, delicate ravioli.

TO SERVE 6

☞ Transparent Ravioli of Fresh Herbs

½ recipe Basic Egg Pasta (page 201), rolled out as thinly as possible and cut into 36 triangles with 2-inch sides
6 small, perfect sprigs fresh cilantro
6 small, perfect sprigs fresh dill
6 small, perfect sprigs fresh sage
1 tablespoon kosher salt
1 large dried red Chimayo chile
9 cups Basic Consommé (page 48)

For the Transparent Ravioli: Place 18 of the pasta triangles on a work surface. Rinse all the fresh herb sprigs and place each one, still moist, on top of a triangle. Dip your finger in cold water and moisten the surface of the pasta. Place 1 of the remaining 18 triangles on top of each herb-covered one, and press gently on their surfaces to seal the ravioli.

In a wide, shallow saucepan over moderate-to-high heat, bring 1½ inches of water and 1 tablespoon of kosher salt to a low rolling boil. Add the ravioli and cook them until transparent and just tender, about 3 minutes. Drain them and set aside.

For the Consommé: Roast the chile over an open flame or under a hot broiler until crisp, about 45 seconds. Remove the seeds and cut it crosswise into ¼-inch slivers. Put the chile slivers and the consommé into a large saucepan over moderate-to-high heat. Bring the consommé to a boil, then reduce the heat and simmer, uncovered, for about 5 minutes.

Pour the consommé and chile slivers into large shallow warmed soup plates. Place one each of the 3 kinds of ravioli into each plate, and serve the soup immediately.

Posole Consommé with Foie Gras and Truffle

In the Southwest the large kernels of dried corn called *posole* are often cooked in broth with salt pork and red chile and eaten as a simple soup. Here I've combined this domestic food with two aristocrats of the French kitchen, foie gras and black truffle, to make an elegant soup with rich, earthy undertones.

Fresh foie gras may be difficult to find, although excellent domestic foie gras now is being produced. If necessary, a good-quality canned foie gras is a respectable substitute. In place of a whole black truffle, you can use canned truffle parings, available in gourmet markets.

Consommé with Transparent Ravioli of Fresh Herbs and Slivered Chile Garnish

TO SERVE 6

9 cups Basic Consommé
 (page 48)
½ cup cooked Posole (page 196)
1 large black truffle, scrubbed,
 thinly sliced
4 ounces foie gras, cut into strips
 3 inches long and ¼ inch wide
 and thick

Put the consommé, posole and truffle in a large saucepan. Bring the consommé to a boil over moderate-to-high heat; reduce the heat and simmer the soup briskly, uncovered, for about 5 minutes.

Distribute the pieces of foie gras in large, shallow warmed soup plates. Ladle the consommé, with the posole and truffles, into each plate and serve immediately.

TWO SOUPS IN ONE BOWL

Guests at Saint Estèphe are delighted when we serve two soups of contrasting, but complementary, flavors and colors, side by side in the same bowl. It looks difficult; but actually all it takes is a pair of thick soups that have the same consistency, two equal-sized ladles, and steady hands for pouring them simultaneously.

Fill each ladle with one of the soups and hold them at opposite sides of a large, shallow soup plate. Pour slowly from the ladles simultaneously, until the bottom of the bowl is covered and the soups meet in the middle, moving the ladles as you pour so the soups flow together and touch in a fairly even line. Then continue pouring, adjusting the pouring motion to keep the two soups at the same level.

Any one of the six Modern Southwest-style soups recipes that follow is delicious served on its own. But I've created them to be paired up, and if you serve two in one bowl you should only make a half recipe of each soup. Garnish the soups with a fresh herb—dill for the green and red tomato soups; a sprig of cilantro for the green and yellow squash soups; and fresh chives to go with the pinto and white bean soups.

Posole Consommé with Foie Gras and Truffle

Green Tomato and Green Chile Soup

7 tablespoons unsalted butter
2 medium-size russet potatoes, peeled and cut into ¼-inch dice
2 medium onions, coarsely chopped
1 fresh green Anaheim chile, stemmed, seeded and coarsely chopped
1 bay leaf
1 teaspoon dried thyme
1 dozen medium-size green tomatoes, coarsely chopped
1 cup Chicken Stock (page 211)
2 cups half-and-half
1 teaspoon salt
1 teaspoon white pepper
6 small sprigs fresh dill, for garnish

Melt 4 tablespoons of the butter in a medium saucepan over moderate-to-high heat. Add the potatoes and sauté them for about 5 minutes; then add the onions, chile, bay leaf and thyme and sauté about 2 minutes more.

Add the tomatoes and the chicken stock. Bring the liquid to a boil, then reduce the heat and simmer, uncovered, until the vegetables are tender, about 25 minutes.

Remove the bay leaf from the pan and transfer the contents to a food processor; puree them. Return the puree to the saucepan and add the half-and-half, salt, pepper, and the remaining butter. Stir the soup over moderate heat just until the butter melts and the soup is hot. Sieve the soup and serve it in heated bowls, garnished with sprigs of fresh dill.

Red Tomato and Red Chile Soup

7 tablespoons unsalted butter
2 medium-size russet potatoes, peeled and diced ¼ inch
2 medium onions, coarsely chopped
1 red bell pepper, stemmed, seeded and coarsely chopped
½ teaspoon chile pequín (available in Latin markets)
1 dozen medium-size ripe tomatoes, coarsely chopped
1 cup Chicken Stock (page 211)
2 cups half-and-half
1 teaspoon salt
1 teaspoon white pepper
6 small sprigs fresh dill, for garnish

Melt 4 tablespoons of the butter in a medium saucepan over moderate-to-high heat. Add the potatoes and sauté them for about 5 minutes; then add the onions, bell pepper and chile pequín and sauté about 2 minutes more.

Add the tomatoes and the chicken stock. Bring the liquid to a boil, then reduce the heat and simmer, uncovered, until the vegetables are tender, about 25 minutes.

Transfer the contents of the pan to a processor and puree them. Return the puree to the saucepan and add the half-and-half, salt, pepper, and the remaining butter. Stir the soup over moderate heat, just until the butter melts and the soup is hot. Sieve the soup and serve it in heated bowls, garnished with sprigs of fresh dill.

Two soups in one bowl. Top: *Green Tomato and Green Chile, and Red Tomato and Red Chile* soups. Bottom left: *Pinto Bean and White Bean* soups. Bottom, right: *Green Calabacita and Yellow Calabacita soups*

Green Calabacita Soup

Every fall, my Grandma Eloisa made plenty of the homestyle vegetable dish called *calabacita*—a mixture of zucchini, corn, green chiles, onions and garlic, a kind of Southwestern *ratatouille*. That traditional dish was the inspiration for this smoothly pureed soup.

TO SERVE 6

4 tablespoons unsalted butter
2 medium-size russet potatoes, peeled and cut into ½-inch dice
2 medium onions, coarsely chopped
2 medium garlic cloves, finely chopped
1 fresh green Anaheim chile, stemmed, seeded and coarsely chopped
1 bay leaf
½ teaspoon dried thyme
9 medium zucchini, coarsely chopped
3 cups Chicken Stock (page 211)
½ cup pumpkin seeds, shelled and toasted (page 24)
2 cups half-and-half
½ teaspoon salt
½ teaspoon white pepper
6 sprigs fresh cilantro, for garnish

Melt the butter in a medium saucepan over moderate-to-high heat. Add the potatoes and sauté them for about 5 minutes; then add the onions, garlic, chile and herbs and sauté about 2 minutes more.

Add the zucchini and the chicken stock. Bring the liquid to a boil, then reduce the heat and simmer, uncovered, until the vegetables are tender, about 20 minutes.

Remove the bay leaf from the pan. Transfer the contents of the pan to a processor, add the pumpkin seeds, and puree the soup. Return the puree to the saucepan and add the half-and-half, salt and pepper. Stir the soup over moderate heat, just until it is hot. Sieve the soup and serve it in heated bowls, garnished with cilantro.

Yellow Calabacita Soup

Golden-colored squash gives a unique sweet flavor to this soup.

TO SERVE 6

Melt the butter in a medium saucepan over moderate-to-high heat. Add the potatoes and sauté them for about 5 minutes; then add the onions, chile and herbs and sauté about 2 minutes more.

Add the squash and the chicken stock. Bring the liquid to a boil, then reduce the heat and simmer until the vegetables are tender, about 20 minutes.

Remove the bay leaf from the pan. Transfer the contents of the pan to a processor, add the pine nuts, and puree the soup. Return the puree to the saucepan and add the half-and-half, salt and pepper. Stir the soup over moderate heat, just until it is hot. Sieve the soup and serve it in heated bowls, garnished with cilantro.

4 tablespoons unsalted butter
2 medium-size russet potatoes, peeled and cut into ½-inch dice
2 medium onions, coarsely chopped
1 bay leaf
½ teaspoon dried thyme
1 dozen medium-size yellow squash, coarsely chopped
3 cups Chicken Stock (page 211)
½ cup pine nuts, toasted (page 24)
2 cups half-and-half
½ teaspoon white pepper
6 sprigs fresh cilantro, for garnish

Pinto Bean Soup

TO SERVE 6

In a large saucepan, bring the water to a boil over moderate-to-high heat. Add the beans, bacon, garlic, onion, bay leaf and thyme. Reduce the heat to a simmer, cover the pan and cook until the beans are tender, about 3½ hours, adding a little more water if necessary to keep the beans covered.

Remove the bacon or salt pork and the bay leaf from the pan. Pour the contents of the pan into a processor and puree them. Return the puree to the pan over moderate heat, stir in the half-and-half, salt and pepper, and cook until the soup is just heated through, about 5 minutes. Sieve the soup and serve it immediately in heated bowls, garnished with fresh chives.

3 quarts water
1 cup dried pinto beans, washed in cold running water
¼ pound piece of bacon or salt pork, cut in half
3 medium garlic cloves, peeled and left whole
1 small onion, peeled and quartered
1 bay leaf
½ teaspoon dried thyme
3 cups half-and-half
½ teaspoon salt
½ teaspoon white pepper
Fresh chives, for garnish

White Bean Soup

TO SERVE 6

3 quarts water
1 cup dried Great Northern
   beans, washed in cold running
   water
¼ pound bacon or salt pork cut
   in half
3 medium garlic cloves, peeled
   and left whole
1 small onion, peeled and
   quartered
1 bay leaf
1 teaspoon chile pequín
   (available in Latin markets)
3 cups half-and-half
½ teaspoon salt
½ teaspoon white pepper
   Fresh chives, for garnish

In a large saucepan, bring the water to a boil over moderate-to-high heat. Add the beans, bacon, garlic, onion, bay leaf and chile pequín. Reduce the heat to a simmer, cover the pan and cook until the beans are tender, about 3½ hours, adding a little more water if necessary to keep the beans covered.

Remove the bacon and bay leaf from the pan. Pour the contents of the pan into a processor and puree them. Return the puree to the pan over moderate heat, stir in the half-and-half, salt and pepper, and cook just until the soup is heated through, about 5 minutes. Sieve the soup and serve it immediately in heated bowls, garnished with fresh chives.

Corn Chowder with Tic-tac-toe of Caviars

Chowder may make you think of a chunky, hearty soup. This soup, however, is more like a Southwestern variation on a classic French vichyssoise—a smooth, creamy corn soup, served chilled. Three different kinds of caviar, with their salty tang of the sea, make an elegant garnish for the soup. I like to arrange them playfully in a tic-tac-toe pattern on the bottom of each serving plate, and let each guest pour his or her own portion of soup over the garnish. Finely chopped smoked salmon or vegetables can be substituted for the caviars.

Corn Chowder with Tic-tac-toe of Caviars

TO SERVE 6

≡☞ *Corn Chowder*

5 tablespoons unsalted butter
3 medium leeks, white parts
  only, washed and cut into
  ¼-inch slices
2 large russet potatoes, peeled
  and cut into ½-inch cubes
3 large ears of corn, shucked,
  silk strings removed, kernels
  cut from cobs
2 cups Chicken Stock (page 211)
2 cups half-and-half
½ teaspoon salt
½ teaspoon white pepper

≡☞ *Tic-tac-toe of Caviars*

24 perfect chives, trimmed 4½
  inches long
2 ounces Beluga caviar
1 ounce American golden caviar
  (whitefish roe)
1 ounce salmon caviar
2 tablespoons finely chopped
  fresh chives

For the Corn Chowder: Melt the butter in a large saucepan over moderate heat. Add the leeks and sauté them until soft, about 3 minutes. Add the potatoes and corn and sauté them for about 10 minutes more, stirring frequently. Add the chicken stock, and simmer until the potatoes are tender, about 15 minutes.

Transfer the soup to the processor and puree it, in batches if necessary. Stir in the half-and-half and seasonings, then pass the soup through a sieve. Chill the soup in the refrigerator for at least 3 hours.

For the Tic-tac-toe of Caviars: Bring the small saucepan of water to a boil. Add the trimmed chives and blanch them for just 5 seconds, then rinse them under cold running water.

Place 4 chives in each large shallow soup plate to make the grid of a tic-tac-toe game. With a teaspoon, shape an "X" of Beluga caviar in the top left and lower right corners of each grid; shape an "O" of golden caviar in the center square of each grid; shape an "X" of salmon caviar in the lower left corner; and an "X" of chopped chives in the top center space. Chill the plates in the refrigerator for 30 minutes.

To serve the soup, place a garnished soup plate in front of each guest. Serve the chilled soup from the tureen or from individual pitchers at table, for each guest to pour over the tic-tac-toe pattern.

Soup of Quail Egg Huevos Rancheros

Two of my favorite traditional Southwestern dishes are combined in this new Southwestern soup. The tortilla soups I used to eat in Santa Fe were chile-flavored red bean or pinto bean soups thickened with crumbled tortilla chips and topped with grated Cheddar cheese; in this soup, strips of corn tortilla and sharp Cheddar cheese are arranged to make "nests" in large soup bowls.

Each nest holds a pair of gently fried quail eggs—a refined version of heuvos rancheros in combination with the tortillas, the cheese and the thick, spicy tomatillo soup poured into the bowls at table. Quail eggs are available

Soup of Quail Egg Huevos Rancheros

in many gourmet food stores. Buy 6 more than the dozen called for in the recipe: their soft shells and the tough membranes that line their interiors are awkward to open, and you may break a few yolks in the process. If quail eggs are unavailable, substitute one hen's egg per serving.

TO SERVE 6

☞ *Tomatillo Soup*

4 tablespoons unsalted butter
1 russet potato, peeled and cut into ¼-inch dice
4 large garlic cloves, finely chopped
3 fresh green Anaheim chiles, stemmed, seeded, coarsely chopped
1 large onion, coarsely chopped
1 bay leaf
1 teaspoon fresh oregano leaves, finely chopped (or ½ teaspoon dried oregano)
2 dozen tomatillos, husked and coarsely chopped
1 cup Chicken Stock (page 211)
½ teaspoon salt
½ teaspoon white pepper

☞ *Quail Egg Heuvos Rancheros*

3 gold corn tortillas
Vegetable oil for frying
6 ounces sharp Cheddar cheese
12 or more quail eggs (see above)

For the Tomatillo Soup: Melt the butter in a medium saucepan over moderate-to-high heat. Add the potato and sauté it for about 5 minutes; then add the garlic, chiles, onion and herbs and sauté about 2 minutes more.

Add the tomatillos, chicken stock, salt and pepper. Bring the liquid to a boil, then reduce the heat and simmer until the vegetables are tender, about 20 minutes.

For the Quail Egg Huevos Rancheros: While the soup is simmering, prepare the nests and quail eggs. Cut the tortillas in half, then cut each half crosswise into ¼-inch strips. Heat ½ inch of oil in a heavy skillet to a temperature of 425°F. on a deep-frying thermometer. Add the tortilla strips and fry them until crisp, about 2 minutes. Remove them with a skimmer; drain them on paper towels and pat them dry.

Cut the cheese into strips 3 inches long and ¼ inch wide and thick. Lay cheese and tortilla strips in a random crisscross pattern on the bottom of 6 large, deep soup bowls to make the circular bases of the nests, then lay the remaining strips around the edges of the circles to make wide sides to the nests. Set the bowls aside.

Heat ¼ inch of oil in another skillet over moderate heat. One at a time, gently pierce the side of each quail egg by carefully pinching it with your fingernails; then, directly over the surface of the oil tear it open and empty the egg into the skillet. Gently fry the eggs just until their whites are set and firm, about 1½ minutes. Carefully remove the fried eggs with a thin spatula and drain them on paper towels. Transfer 2 eggs to the center of each nest.

Remove the bay leaf from the soup pan. Transfer the soup to a processor and puree it. Pass the soup through a sieve. Return it to the saucepan and cook it over moderate heat until hot, about 3 minutes.

Place a soup bowl with its nest of quail eggs in front of each guest. Serve the soup from a tureen or from individual pitchers at table, for each guest to pour over the nest.

CHAPTER 3

APPETIZERS

Salmon Mousse Tamales with Ground Nixtamal and Cilantro Cream Sauce

TO SERVE 6

▼◻ Salmon Mousse Tamales

1½ pounds fresh salmon, trimmed of all ligaments, membrane and fat, cut into chunks

2 cups heavy cream

1 teaspoon salt

1 teaspoon white pepper

1 egg

6 ounces Nixtamal (page 23)

6 perfect watercress sprigs

12 dried corn husks (available at Latin markets; or use husks from fresh ears)

¼ cup fresh corn kernels, parboiled, for garnish

2 medium tomatoes, peeled, seeded and diced, for garnish

▼◻ Cilantro Cream Sauce

1 teaspoon unsalted butter

2 medium shallots, finely chopped

½ cup dry white wine

1 tablespoon red wine vinegar

½ teaspoon salt

½ teaspoon white pepper

2 cups heavy cream

1 tablespoon finely chopped cilantro

For the Salmon Mousse Tamales: Put the salmon, cream, salt and pepper in a processor and process for about 1 minute, stopping a few times to scrape down the bowl. Add the egg and process 1 minute more, to make a firm, dense mousse mixture. It should be free of any ligaments or fat; if any are visible, press the mixture with a rubber spatula through a fine sieve.

For each tamale, place a 4- by 5-inch sheet of plastic wrap on the work surface. Spread a ¼-inch-thick layer of nixtamal in a 1½- by 3-inch rectangle in the center of the sheet. On top of the nixtamal, spread a ½-inch-thick layer of the mousse mixture. Place a sprig of watercress on top of the mousse. Cut a 1½- by 3-inch rectangle from each of 6 corn husks and place it on top. Bring the plastic wrap up and around the husk to seal the tamale in a neat package. Set the tamales aside.

For the Cilantro Cream Sauce: Melt the butter in a large saucepan over moderate heat. Add the shallots and sauté them for about 3 minutes, until translucent. Add the wine, vinegar, salt and pepper and simmer until reduced by half, about 10 minutes. Add the cream and continue simmering, stirring frequently, for 15 to 20 minutes, until the sauce reduces to about 1 cup and has a light, creamy consistency. Pass the sauce through a sieve. Stir in the cilantro and keep the sauce warm.

Bring an inch or so of water to a boil in a steamer or a large pot with a steaming rack. Steam the tamales for 7 to 8 minutes, until firm to the touch.

While the tamales are steaming, take the remaining 6 pieces of husk and tie one end of each husk in a knot, to make a boatlike shape.

Unwrap the plastic wrap from each tamale. Lift the corn husk off of the salmon mousse. Carefully place the tamale on top of a corn-husk boat with the salmon mousse side up.

Spread 3 tablespoons of sauce in the middle of each serving plate. Place a tamale on top, spoon a little more sauce inside the husk, and garnish with a sprinkling of corn kernels and diced tomato.

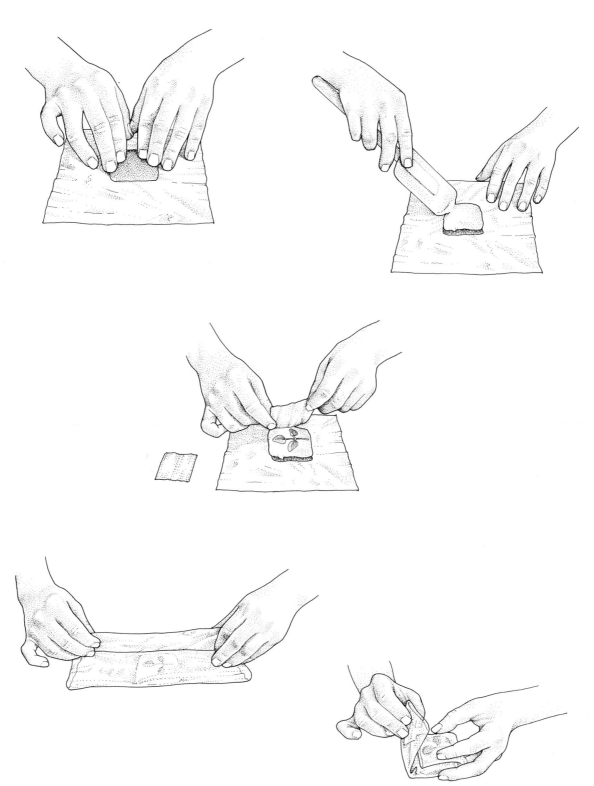

Once the top piece of corn husk is in place, the tamale is prepared for steaming.

Spinach Tamales with Anchovy Sauce

A briny sauce of anchovies is frequently served with soufflés of spinach. Here it accompanies tamales filled with a light mixture of spinach, eggs and cream.

TO SERVE 6

For the Spinach Tamales: Bring 2 quarts of water to a boil with 2 tablespoons of kosher salt in a medium saucepan. Add the spinach and cook it for 1 minute. Drain well and let the spinach cool.

While the spinach cools, melt the butter in a small skillet over moderate heat. Add the diced red pepper and ½ teaspoon of the white pepper and sauté for about 2 minutes, until the pepper is crisp-tender. Set it aside.

Using your hands, squeeze as much excess water from the spinach as possible. Put the spinach in a processor and puree it. Add the eggs, cream, remaining salt and remaining white pepper and pulse until well blended. Remove the spinach mixture from the processor and fold in the diced red pepper.

For each of the 6 tamales, place a 4- by 5-inch sheet of plastic wrap on the work surface. Spread a ¼-inch-thick layer of nixtamal in a 1½- by 3-inch rectangle in the center of each sheet. Divide the spinach mixture, spreading it over the nixtamal. Cut a 1½- by 3-inch rectangle from each of 6 corn husks and place it on top of the spinach. Bring the plastic wrap up and around the husk to seal the tamale in a neat package. (See illustration for Salmon Mousse Tamales, page 67). Set the tamales aside.

For the Anchovy Sauce: Put the cream, anchovies, tomato and 1 teaspoon of the white pepper in a medium saucepan and bring to a boil over moderate-to-high heat. Reduce the heat to maintain a low rolling boil and cook the sauce, stirring occasionally, until it has reduced to 1½ cups, about 25 minutes. Transfer the sauce to a processor and pulse it a few times until smooth, then pass it through a sieve and keep it warm.

Bring a small amount of water to a boil in a steamer or a large pot with a steaming rack. Steam the tamales for 7 to 8 minutes, until firm to the touch.

Spinach Tamales

7 bunches spinach, washed and stemmed
2 tablespoons kosher salt
1 tablespoon unsalted butter
1 medium-size red bell pepper, stemmed, seeded and cut into ¼-inch dice
1 teaspoon white pepper
4 eggs
½ cup heavy cream
½ teaspoon salt
6 ounces Nixtamal (page 23)
12 dried corn husks (available in Latin markets, or use fresh corn husks)

Anchovy Sauce

3 cups heavy cream
⅓ cup anchovy fillets (8 to 12 fillets), rinsed well
1 large tomato, peeled, seeded and cut into ¼-inch dice
1⅛ teaspoons white pepper
1 teaspoon unsalted butter
1 large red bell pepper, stemmed, seeded and cut into ¼-inch dice
⅛ teaspoon salt

Tamales. Top: Tamale of Sweetbreads with Morels and Black Truffle. Center, left: Japanese Tamales of Pompano with Ginger Butter. Center, right: Spinach Tamale with Anchovy Sauce. Bottom: Salmon Mousse Tamale with Ground Nixtamal and Cilantro Cream Sauce

While the tamales are steaming, take the remaining 6 pieces of husk and tie one end of each husk in a knot, to make a boatlike shape.

Melt the butter in a small saucepan and add the bell pepper dice, the remaining white pepper and the salt. Sauté the bell pepper dice for 2 to 3 minutes, just until they are heated.

Unwrap the plastic wrap from each tamale. Lift the corn husk off the spinach mousse. Carefully place the tamale on top of a corn-husk boat with the spinach side up.

Spoon the sauce into the middle of each large warmed serving plate. Place the tamale on top and spoon a little more sauce inside the husk boat. Sprinkle the diced bell pepper over the sauce.

Tamales of Sweetbreads with Morels and Black Truffle

I think this makes the most delicately flavored and beautiful tamales—a light mousse of chicken breast studded with pieces of sweetbread and slivers of black truffle, served with a rich Madeira sauce and garnished with truffles, morels and fresh corn kernels. The luxurious ingredients indicate a very special dish.

TO SERVE 6

◀ Tamales of Sweetbreads

9 ounces veal sweetbreads
10 ounces skinless, boned chicken breast, cut into 3 or 4 pieces
1 teaspoon salt
1 teaspoon white pepper
¾ cup heavy cream
1 egg
1 egg white
1 ounce black truffle (whole or peelings), cut into thin slivers about ¼ inch long
6 ounces Nixtamal (page 23)

For the Tamales of Sweetbreads: Bring 2 quarts of water with ½ tablespoon of salt to a boil in a large saucepan. Reduce the heat, carefully slip in the sweetbreads and cook them for 30 minutes.

When the sweetbreads are almost done, prepare a bowl of ice water. Drain the sweetbreads and plunge them quickly into the ice water to stop the cooking. Carefully pull off any clear membrane from the sweetbreads. Cut sweetbreads into ½-inch pieces. Set them aside.

Put the pieces of chicken breast, salt and pepper in a processor and pulse several times until coarsely chopped, then process until smooth. Pulse in the cream, egg and egg white, just until well blended. Remove the mixture from the processor and gently fold into it the sweetbread pieces and ¾ of the slivered truffle.

For each of the 6 tamales, place a 4- by 5-inch sheet of plastic wrap on the work surface. Spread a ¼-inch-thick layer of nixtamal in a 1½- by 3-inch rectangle in the center of each sheet. On top of the nixtamal, spread the sweetbread mixture, dividing it equally among the 6 rectangles. Cut a 1½- by 3-inch rectangle from each of 6 corn husks and place on top of each tamale. Bring the plastic wrap up and around the husk to seal the tamale in a neat package. (See illustration for Salmon Mousse Tamales, page 67). Set the tamales aside.

For the Madeira Sauce: Put the cream, stock and Madeira in a medium saucepan and bring mixture to a boil over moderate-to-high heat. Reduce the heat and simmer briskly until reduced to 1½ cups, 15 to 20 minutes.

Meanwhile, bring water to a boil in a steamer or a large pot with a steaming rack. Steam the tamales for 7 to 8 minutes, until firm to the touch.

For the Garnish: While the tamales are steaming, melt the butter in a small saucepan over moderate heat. Add the corn, morels and the reserved truffle slivers and sauté them for about 2 minutes, just until heated through.

Take the remaining 6 pieces of husk and tie one end of each husk in a knot, to make a boatlike shape.

Unwrap the plastic wrap from each tamale. Lift off the rectangle of corn husk. Carefully place the tamale on top of a corn-husk boat with the sweetbread mixture side up, then place a tamale boat in the center of each large warmed serving plate. Spoon the sauce around and inside the husk, and sprinkle it with the corn, morels and truffles.

12 dried corn husks (available in Latin markets; or use husks from fresh ears)

◥ *Madeira Sauce*
 2 cups heavy cream
 1 cup Veal Stock (page 212)
 ¼ cup Madeira

◥ *Garnish*
 1 tablespoon unsalted butter
 ½ cup cooked corn kernels
 4 ounces small fresh morels, or 1 ounce dried morels soaked for about 15 minutes in warm water and drained, halved lengthwise

Japanese Tamales of Pompano with Ginger Butter

Tamales are defined as much by the use of corn husks for the steaming vessel as they are by the presence of nixtamal, the corn mush filling. In this recipe, nixtamal is replaced by cooked rice, as a base for small whole fish that are topped with fresh corn and, for a Japanese touch, seaweed.

◤◳ *Japanese Tamales of Pompano*

¼ cup short-grain glutinous rice, rinsed

2 fresh jalapeño chiles, stemmed, seeded and coarsely chopped

½ red bell pepper, seeded and coarsely chopped

1 tablespoon kosher salt

2 quarts water

2 ears of corn, shucked, strings removed, kernels cut from cobs

13 dried corn husks (available in Latin markets; or husks from fresh ears may be used), soaked in warm water for 10 minutes

6 small Florida pompano or small perch, cleaned, left whole

1 teaspoon salt

1 teaspoon white pepper

2 tomatoes, peeled, seeded and cut into ¼-inch dice

6 ounces edible seaweed (available from Japanese markets) cut into ¼-inch strips

◤◳ *Ginger Butter*

½ cup rice vinegar

4 tablespoons chopped preserved ginger in syrup

1½ cups heavy cream

8 tablespoons unsalted butter, cut into small pieces

For the Japanese Tamales of Pompano: Put the rice, chiles and bell pepper in a small saucepan and add enough cold water to cover them by about ½ inch. Bring to a boil over moderate heat, stir once, then cover the pan, reduce the heat and simmer until all the liquid has been absorbed, about 15 minutes. Remove the pan from the heat and let it sit, covered, for about 10 minutes. Stir the rice briefly with a 2-pronged fork, cover it again and let it sit for 10 minutes more. Uncover the pan and let the rice cool to room temperature.

While the rice is cooling, bring 2 quarts of water to a boil with 1 tablespoon of kosher salt in a medium saucepan. Add the corn kernels and cook them for 5 minutes, then rinse them under cold running water and drain well.

Place 6 corn husks on the work surface. Spread the rice in the center of each husk in a 2- by 3-inch rectangle about ¼ inch thick. Season the pompano with salt and white pepper and place them on top of the rice. Top the fish with the corn, tomatoes and seaweed.

Wrap the ends and sides of the corn husk around the filling in a tidy package. Place each package, folded side down, on top of another corn husk and fold the husk around the package. Tear thin strips from the remaining corn husk and use them to tie each tamale securely. (See illustration for Salmon Mousse Tamales, page 67).

Bring water to a boil in a steamer or a large pot with a steaming rack. Steam the tamales for 15 minutes.

For the Ginger Butter: While the tamales are steaming, bring the vinegar to a boil in a small saucepan over moderate-to-high heat. Boil the vinegar until it reduces to ¼ cup, about 5 minutes. Add the ginger and cream and cook the sauce at a low rolling boil until it reduces to 1 cup, about 10 minutes more.

As soon as the tamales are done, whisk the butter, a few pieces at a time, into the ginger-cream mixture. Sieve the sauce and keep it warm.

Unwrap the outer husk from each tamale, and unfold the inner husk in the middle of each large warmed serving plate to reveal the fish. Spoon the ginger butter around each tamale on the plate, and spoon a little more sauce inside the husk.

Escargot Enchiladas with Port Wine Sauce and Spinach

Fresh American snails are now being raised in the Sonoma Valley, part of California's wine country but they are not yet widely available; however, imported canned French escargots from Burgundy are fine for this recipe and only need to be warmed through before serving.

TO SERVE 6

For the Port Wine Sauce: Bring the port and veal stock to a boil in a saucepan over moderate-to-high heat. Cook on a low rolling boil until reduced to 1½ cups, about 25 minutes, then whisk in the butter. Remove the sauce from the heat and keep it warm.

For the Escargot Enchiladas: While the sauce is reducing, prepare the enchiladas. Bring 2 quarts of water to a boil with 2 teaspoons of kosher salt in a large saucepan. Plunge the spinach into the water, then immediately drain it and let it cool. With your hands, squeeze out all excess water from the spinach. Put the spinach in a processor and puree it. Melt the butter in a small sauté pan over moderate heat, add the spinach, salt and pepper, and warm the spinach puree through. Keep it warm.

Stacking the tortillas 2 at a time, use the tip of a small sharp knife to cut out the largest triangles possible from each tortilla. Cut each triangle in half to make 2 equal triangles (reserve the trimmings for tortilla chips or confetti of tortilla—page 197). In a large heavy skillet, heat ½ inch of oil to 375°F. on a deep-frying thermometer. Fry the tortillas for about 30 seconds, until tender, soft and flexible. Pat them dry with paper towels and set them aside.

Transfer the reduced sauce to a small sauté pan over moderate heat and add the snails. Bring the sauce to a boil and cook for just a few minutes, until the snails are heated through.

Spoon the sauce into the middle of each of 6 large warmed serving plates. Place a tortilla triangle along the side of the sauce and spoon some of the spinach puree on top. Scatter 6 snails randomly on the plate, 2 or 3 of them on top of the spinach and the rest on the sauce. Place another triangle on top of the spinach. Decorate the rim of the sauce with a sprinkling of tarragon leaves.

Port Wine Sauce
2 cups port
1 cup concentrated Veal Stock (page 212)
2 tablespoons unsalted butter

Escargot Enchiladas
2 teaspoons kosher salt
3 bunches spinach, washed and stemmed
1 tablespoon butter
⅛ teaspoon salt
⅛ teaspoon white pepper
6 6-inch blue corn tortillas
Vegetable oil for deep frying
36 large snails (about 6 ounces total weight)
1 bunch fresh tarragon unblemished leaves plucked and reserved

Gratin of Oysters with Blue and Gold Cornbread Crumbs

Gratin is French for "crust," and today most people think of gratins as dishes topped with a crust of cheese or breadcrumbs. But originally, gratins were oven-baked dishes *lined* with a breadcrumb crust. This Southwestern-style gratin comes closer to those earlier versions, with a crust of blue and gold cornbread crumbs rapidly browned on each individual serving plate as an accompaniment to plump poached oysters and a champagne cream sauce.

TO SERVE 6

◤▫ Cornbread Gratin

1½ cups Blue Cornbread crumbs (see recipe for Blue Cornbread on page 197)
1½ cups Gold Cornbread crumbs (use same recipe as for above, substituting yellow cornmeal for blue)
½ cup unsalted butter, melted

◤▫ Oysters and Sauce

24 large Belon or Malpeque oysters, shucked, liquor reserved
2 cups champagne
1 small shallot, finely chopped
2 cups heavy cream
1 tablespoon unsalted butter
1 large tomato, peeled, seeded and cut into ¼-inch dice
1 tablespoon chopped fresh tarragon

For the Cornbread Gratin: Separately mix the blue cornbread crumbs and the gold cornbread crumbs with ¼ cup each of the melted butter. On each of 6 ovenproof dinner plates, arrange the crumbs in 8 alternating stripes ½ inch wide and 4 inches long, to make a 4-inch square of crumbs. Set the plates aside.

For the Oysters and Sauce: Combine the oyster liquor, champagne and shallot in a medium saucepan and bring to a boil over moderate-to-high heat. Reduce the heat to a simmer, slip in the oysters and poach them for about 3 minutes, just until they plump up and curl at the edges. Remove them to a bowl and keep them warm.

Raise the heat to high and boil the liquid until it reduces to 1 cup, about 10 minutes. Add the cream and continue boiling until the sauce has reduced to 1½ cups. Strain the sauce and keep it warm.

Preheat the broiler.

Melt the tablespoon of butter in a small skillet, add the tomato and tarragon and sauté for 2 to 3 minutes, just until heated through. Set the skillet aside.

Put the plates under the hot broiler for about 30 seconds, just long enough to brown the gratins slightly around the edges; take care not to let them burn. Carefully remove the plates and spoon the sauce around the sides of the gratin. Place 4 oysters on each plate, on top of the sauce and one at each side of the gratin square. Sprinkle a little of the tomato-tarragon mixture on top of each oyster.

Gratin of Oysters with Blue and Gold Cornbread Crumbs

Sea Urchins with Blue Cornmeal Pasta

I like to think of this dish as the ultimate magical combination of land and sea, the earthy, slightly gritty cornmeal pasta mingling with the intense briny flavor of the sea urchins. Roasted Anaheim chiles stirred into the sauce, add additional spark to the dish.

TO SERVE 6

6 medium-large live sea urchins (3 to 4 inches in diameter)
2 teaspoons kosher salt
24 large spinach leaves, washed and stemmed
2 teaspoons kosher salt
1 tablespoon vegetable oil
1 pound Blue Cornmeal Pasta (page 203), rolled out, dried and cut into 6-inch-long, ½-inch-wide noodles
1½ cups heavy cream
½ teaspoon salt
½ teaspoon white pepper
2 Anaheim chiles, roasted, peeled, seeded and diced

Using a kitchen towel to protect your hands from the spines and to keep the spines from breaking, pick up each sea urchin and turn it over to expose its "beak" or mouth. With kitchen scissors, carefully cut from the center of the beak to the edge of the shell, then all the way around the rim in a circle, to expose the inside of the urchin.

Still holding the urchin with the towel, invert it and shake out any foreign matter inside. Then use a spoon to carefully remove the long, triangular bright orange roe that lines the inside. Set aside 6 whole perfect roe sections when you have completed opening all the urchins, and reserve the rest for the sauce. Set the shells aside.

Bring 2 quarts of water to a boil with 2 teaspoons of kosher salt in a medium saucepan. Add the spinach leaves and blanch them for about 10 seconds; then drain them, rinse them well under cold running water, and pat them dry with paper towels.

Line the inside of each sea-urchin shell with 4 spinach leaves, tucking them in so that they just overlap the rim of the urchin.

Bring another 2 quarts of water to a boil with 2 teaspoons kosher salt and 1 tablespoon vegetable oil in a medium saucepan. Add the pasta and cook it until it is tender but still slightly chewy (al dente) about 5 minutes. Drain the pasta well and set it aside.

Put the cream in a processor or blender with all sea-urchin roes except the 6 reserved and process until smooth. Bring the mixture to a boil in a medium saucepan over moderate-to-high heat; then immediately sieve it, return it to the pan and stir in the chiles. Heat the sauce back to the boil and add the pasta, stirring briefly to heat the pasta through.

Place each lined sea-urchin shell in the center of a serving plate. Fill the shells with the pasta and sauce, and top each serving with a perfect section of orange roe.

Sea Urchin with Blue Cornmeal Pasta

Pyramids of Red and Green Chile Pasta Served with a Jalapeño Cream Sauce

In this light appetizer, the pasta sits on top of the sauce—a sharply flavored jalapeño chile cream that nicely offsets the spice of the two differently flavored pastas. You can make the pasta dough well in advance and have it cut out and ready to cook just before serving. At the restaurant we use a simple cardboard cutout as a template for trimming the pasta shapes, which are reminiscent of Aztec pyramid designs.

TO SERVE 6

Jalapeño Cream Sauce
½ cup Jalapeño Vinegar (page 203)
1 medium shallot, finely chopped
½ teaspoon salt
3 cups heavy cream

Pyramids of Red and Green Chile Pasta
4 ounces Red Chile Pasta, rolled out thinly and dried (page 201)
4 ounces Green Chile Pasta, rolled out thinly and dried (page 202)
¼ cup vegetable oil
1 teaspoon kosher salt
¼ cup Red Chile Indian Paint (page 209)

For the Jalapeño Cream Sauce: Put the vinegar, shallot and salt in a medium saucepan over moderate-to-high heat. Boil the vinegar until it reduces by half to ¼ cup, about 5 minutes. Add the cream, bring it to a boil, reduce the heat and maintain a low, rolling boil until the sauce has reduced to 1½ cups, about 25 minutes. Sieve the sauce and keep it warm.

For the Pyramids of Red and Green Chile Pasta: While the sauce is reducing, prepare the pasta pyramids. Cut each sheet of rolled-out red and green pasta into 6 pieces about 3 inches by 6 inches. Stack several pieces of pasta at a time and, using a cardboard cutout as a guide, trim them with the tip of a sharp knife into 3-stepped pyramids.

Bring 3 quarts of water to a rolling boil with the oil and the salt. Add the red pasta shapes. After 2 minutes, add the green. After 1 minute more (3 minutes total for the red, 2 minutes for the green), remove both pastas with a slotted spoon and drain on paper towels.

Spoon the sauce into the middle of each large warmed serving plate. Place a red and green pasta pyramid on each plate, with their wide bases facing each other about 1 inch apart. Put the Red Chile Indian Paint in a small plastic squeeze bottle and paint 3 evenly spaced dots between the pyramids.

Pyramids of Red and Green Chile Pasta Served with a Jalapeño Cream Sauce

Ravioli of Carne Adobada with Garlic Cream Sauce

In the Southwest, *carne adobada* was originally meat (*carne*) preserved in a pickling brine (*adobo*). The brine, naturally, included a lot of chile and garlic, and the name eventually evolved to mean any meat stewed or seasoned with those spices. Traditionally, the meat is pork chops. But I've found that a carne adobada of shredded pork makes an excellent filling for ravioli. Served with a creamy garlic-flavored sauce, these ravioli have become a very popular appetizer at Saint Estèphe.

TO SERVE 6

◣◻ Ravioli

1 pound boneless pork
1 small onion, coarsely chopped
½ medium carrot, coarsely chopped
½ celery stalk, coarsely chopped
1 small bay leaf, crumbled
½ teaspoon thyme
3 cups water
¼ cup red chile powder
1 large garlic clove, finely chopped
½ teaspoon dried oregano
½ teaspoon salt
½ teaspoon black pepper
1½ pounds Egg Pasta (page 201)

◣◻ Garlic Cream Sauce

1 tablespoon clarified butter
4 large garlic cloves, finely chopped
3 cups heavy cream
1 large shallot, finely chopped
1 teaspoon salt
1 teaspoon white pepper

For the Ravioli: Preheat the oven to 350°F. Put the pork in a roasting pan with the onion, carrot and celery. Sprinkle the meat with the bay leaf and thyme and add the water. Cover the pan with aluminum foil and roast the pork until tender and well done, about 1½ hours. Set the pork aside. Strain the roasting juices and put them in a bowl in the refrigerator to cool until the fat solidifies on the surface. Remove the fat.

When the pork is cool enough to handle, tear the meat by hand into very fine shreds.

Put the defatted roasting juices in a small saucepan and bring them to a boil over high heat; reduce the heat slightly and simmer briskly until the juices have reduced by about half. Add the chile powder, garlic, oregano, salt and pepper; reduce the heat, and simmer gently, uncovered, for about 10 minutes—much of the liquid will be soaked up by the chile. Add the shredded pork, reduce the heat to low, and cook for about 10 minutes more, stirring occasionally, until the mixture is fairly thick, with no excess liquid. Remove the pan from the heat and let the mixture cool to room temperature.

Roll out the pasta as thinly as possible and let it dry (see page 200). Trim the pasta to 12 even 4- by 5-inch rectangles. With a pizza cutter or a crinkle-edged ravioli wheel, cut each rectangle into 4 equal 1- by 1¼-inch rectangles. Place about 2 teaspoons of the carne adobada filling in the center of each of 24 of the rectangles. Dip your finger in water and moisten the edges of each one; top each with one of the remaining rectangles. Press down around the edges with your fingers, then trim the edges slightly with the cutter or ravioli wheel to ensure a tight seal. Set the ravioli aside.

For the Garlic Cream Sauce: Heat the butter in a medium saucepan over moderate heat. Add the chopped garlic and sauté for about 5 minutes, until tender. Add the remaining ingredients, raise the heat to moderate-to-high, and cook the sauce at a low, rolling boil until it reduces to 1½ cups, about 25 minutes. Sieve the sauce and keep it warm.

In a large saucepan, bring 2 quarts of water to a boil with 1 tablespoon of salt and 3 tablespoons of vegetable oil. Cook the ravioli in 2 batches for about 6 minutes per batch, until the pasta is translucent. Remove the ravioli with a slotted spoon and drain them on paper towels.

Spoon the sauce in the center of each large warmed serving plate and place 4 ravioli on top. Garnish each plate with 4 *chiles del arbol*.

1 tablespoon salt
3 tablespoons vegetable oil
24 dried red *chiles del arbol*
   (page 21)

Napa Cabbage Tacos of Shrimp with Sauce Choron

To fill these cabbage-leaf taco shells, use medium-sized fresh shrimp that weigh about 1 ounce each—preferably Santa Barbara shrimp or Spanish red shrimp from the Mediterranean. If these are unavailable, substitute larger shrimp that have been cut into chunks. I like to serve these delicate tacos with a bright-colored Sauce Choron, a variation on Hollandaise, flavored with tarragon, shallot and tomato.

TO SERVE 6

For the Napa Cabbage Tacos: Bring 2 quarts of water to a boil in a large saucepan with 2 teaspoons of kosher salt. Add the cabbage leaves and blanch them for about 10 seconds. Remove them with a skimmer, keeping the water in the saucepan, and rinse under cold running water until cool. Drain well on paper towels and set them aside.

Cut the carrot in half lengthwise and cut from each half 2 lengthwise slices ⅛ inch thick. Cut each slice into long strips ⅛ inch wide, to make about 18 strips. Blanch the strips in the boiling water just until they are flexible, about 15 seconds, then drain and rinse under cold running water. Drain on paper towels and set aside.

Napa Cabbage Tacos of Shrimp

2 teaspoons kosher salt
1 head napa cabbage, peeled to its heart, 12 6-inch leaves reserved
1 medium carrot
18 fresh medium-sized shrimp (about 1 pound 2 ounces total), peeled, deveined and tails removed
1 teaspoon salt
1 teaspoon white pepper

◥⊐ *Sauce Choron*

2 tablespoons red wine vinegar
2 tablespoons tarragon
1 small shallot, finely chopped
4 egg yolks, at room
     temperature
1 teaspoon lemon juice
1 teaspoon warm water
½ teaspoon salt
½ teaspoon white pepper
1 cup clarified butter
2 tablespoons tomato paste

Salt and pepper the raw shrimp.

Bring water to a boil in a steamer or a pot with a steaming rack. Steam the shrimp for about 4 minutes; then pat dry with paper towels. Cut them in half lengthwise, then cut the halves into ¼-inch pieces.

Divide the shrimp among the 12 cabbage leaves, placing them in the center of each leaf. Tuck the top and bottom of each leaf over the shrimp and fold the sides over tightly to enclose them like a package. Turn the tacos, folded side down, and tie each with a strip of carrot (there are extra strips in case some break). Set the tacos aside.

For the Sauce Choron: Put the vinegar, tarragon and shallot in a small saucepan over moderate heat and cook just until the vinegar is absorbed, about 3 minutes. Set aside.

Put the egg yolks, lemon juice, water, salt and pepper in a processor or blender and process them until the yolks are frothy and lemon-colored. With the machine running, slowly pour in the butter in a thin stream, increasing the flow gradually as the sauce thickens. Then pulse in the tarragon-shallot mixture and the tomato concentrate, just until well blended.

Spoon the sauce into the center of each of six large serving plates and place 2 tacos side by side in the center. Serve at room temperature.

Butter Lettuce Tacos of Escargots with Garlic Cream Sauce

Snails with garlic, parsley and butter, with plenty of bread for soaking up the sauce, is a classic combination. In this variation, I wrap a mixture of snails, breadcrumbs, parsley and shallots inside tender leaves of butter lettuce, taco-style. The tacos are then served on top of a rich garlic-flavored cream sauce, and are to be eaten with a fork and knife.

Top: *Red Cabbage Tacos of Duck with Juniper Berry Sauce.* Bottom, left: *Butter Lettuce Tacos of Escargots with Garlic Cream Sauce.* Bottom, right: *Napa Cabbage Tacos of Shrimp with Sauce Choron*

TO SERVE 6

▼⊐ *Butter Lettuce Tacos of Escargots*

1 large red bell pepper
36 large (canned) snails (about 6 ounces total), rinsed
3 slices fresh white bread, crusts removed, finely crumbled
3 large shallots, finely chopped
1 bunch parsley, finely chopped
3 tablespoons unsalted butter, softened
1 teaspoon salt
1 teaspoon white pepper
12 perfect leaves of butter lettuce

▼⊐ *Garlic Cream Sauce*

3 cups heavy cream
3 large garlic cloves, finely chopped
1 teaspoon salt
1 teaspoon white pepper

For the Butter Lettuce Tacos of Escargots: Cut the pepper crosswise into 16 rings about ⅛ inch thick. Remove any seeds from the rings and cut them open to make long strips. Bring a small saucepan of water to a boil and blanch the pepper strips for about 45 seconds, until flexible, then drain them well on paper towels and set the strips aside.

Toss the snails together with the breadcrumbs, shallots, parsley, butter, salt and pepper. Spoon 3 snails with their crumb mixture inside each lettuce leaf. Tuck the top and bottom of each leaf over the snails and fold the sides over tightly to enclose them in a neat package. Turn the tacos folded side down and tie each with a strip of pepper (there are extra strips in case some break). Place the tacos on a buttered baking sheet and set them aside.

For the Garlic Cream Sauce: Put the cream, garlic, salt and pepper in a medium saucepan and bring them to a boil over moderate-to-high heat. Reduce the heat and simmer briskly until the sauce has reduced to 1½ cups, about 12 minutes. Strain the sauce and keep it warm.

Preheat the oven to 425°F. Cover the tacos with a damp kitchen towel and bake them until heated through, about 10 minutes.

Spoon the sauce in a circle in the middle of each of six large heated serving plates. Place 2 tacos side by side on top of the sauce.

Red Cabbage Tacos of Duck with Juniper Berry Sauce

The full, rich flavors of red cabbage and duck make them good partners in a dish. Juniper berries, a traditional seasoning for cabbage, particularly in Alsatian cuisine, give a sharp accent to the sauce that accompanies these tacos. The duck leg meat is robustly flavored after 24 hours of seasoning. Reserve the rest of the ducks for another recipe.

TO SERVE 6

For the Red Cabbage Tacos of Duck: Rub the duck legs with the garlic cloves. Season them with the bay leaf, thyme and pepper and put them in a small bowl. Cover and set in the refrigerator overnight.

Put the duck legs in a small saucepan with the wine and shallots. Bring the wine to a boil over moderate-to-high heat, then reduce the heat and simmer the duck legs until the meat almost falls from the bones, about 45 minutes.

Drain the duck legs and let them cool. (The liquid can be used to replace all or part of the stock called for in the Juniper Berry Sauce.) Pull off and discard the skin and tear the meat into shreds. (The bones can be used for duck stock.)

Melt the butter in a small skillet over moderate heat and sauté the sage and pine nuts until the nuts are golden brown, about 4 minutes. Toss the duck shreds together with the pine nuts and sage and set the mixture aside.

Bring 2 quarts of water and 2 teaspoons of kosher salt to a boil in a medium saucepan. Cut the celery stalks lengthwise into ribbons about ⅛ to ¼ inch thick, making about 16 ribbons in all. Blanch the celery ribbons in the boiling water for about 10 seconds, then lift them out with a slotted spoon and drain them on paper towels. Add the cabbage leaves to the water and blanch for about 20 seconds; drain well and pat dry with paper towels.

Spoon the duck mixture into the middle of each cabbage leaf. Tuck the top and bottom of the leaf over the filling, then fold the sides over tightly to enclose the filling like a package. Turn the tacos folded side down and tie each with a ribbon of celery (There are extra strips in case some break). Place the tacos on a buttered baking sheet and set them aside.

For the Juniper Berry Sauce: Put the wine, stock, juniper berries, thyme and bay leaf in a medium saucepan over moderate-to-high heat. Bring them to a boil, then lower the heat and simmer briskly until the sauce is reduced to 1½ cups. Strain the sauce and keep it warm.

Preheat the oven to 425°F. Cover the tacos with a damp kitchen towel and bake them until heated through, about 8 minutes.

Spoon the sauce in a circle in the middle of each large heated serving plate. Place 2 tacos side by side on top of the sauce.

◀ Red Cabbage Tacos of Duck

3 duck legs
2 large garlic cloves, quartered
2 bay leaves, crumbled
1 tablespoon dried thyme
1 teaspoon black pepper
3 cups dry red wine
2 whole shallots, peeled
1 teaspoon butter
6 fresh sage leaves, shredded
¼ cup pine nuts
2 teaspoons kosher salt
2 celery stalks, strings removed with potato peeler
12 medium-size perfect red cabbage leaves

◀ Juniper Berry Sauce

1½ cups dry red wine
1½ cups Duck Stock (page 212) or concentrated Veal Stock (page 212)
1 tablespoon juniper berries, crushed (wrap them in a towel and hit them with a heavy skillet or kitchen mallet)
1 teaspoon dried thyme
1 bay leaf

Cassolette of Sweetbreads, Pinto Beans and Wild Rice

One of the dishes I remember best from when I was growing up is a big bowl of steaming pinto beans cooked with bacon and garlic and spices. In this recipe I've transformed the beans into an earthy accompaniment for a refined appetizer—sweetbreads, the *ris de veau* of French cuisine. *Cassolette* is a French name for an individual serving dish, like a small pan, used for entrees or hors d'oeuvres. Any small individual serving dish will do.

TO SERVE 6

Pinto Beans

4 quarts water
1 cup dried pinto beans, washed
6 ounces bacon or salt pork, cut into ¼-inch pieces
1 garlic clove, finely chopped

Sweetbreads and Wild Rice

2 cups water
1 teaspoon salt
1 cup wild rice
12 ounces veal sweetbreads
1 teaspoon white pepper

For the Pinto Beans: In a large saucepan, bring the water to a boil. Add the beans, bacon and garlic, reduce the heat and simmer for about 3½ hours or until the beans are tender and their liquid has a thick consistency.

For the sweetbreads and rice: An hour or more before serving, bring the 2 cups of water to a boil and add the wild rice. Reduce the heat, cover and simmer the rice about 40 minutes or until tender and fluffy. Drain rice and keep warm.

At the same time you start boiling water for the rice, bring another large pot of water and one teaspoon of salt to a boil. Reduce the heat, carefully slip in the sweetbreads and cook them for 30 minutes.

When the sweetbreads are almost done, prepare a large bowl of ice water. Drain the sweetbreads and plunge them quickly into the ice water to stop the cooking. Carefully pull off any clear membrane and veins and cut the sweetbreads into ½-inch thick pieces.

Season the sweetbread slices with pepper. Bring water to a boil in a steamer or a large pot with a steaming rack. Steam the sweetbreads until warmed through, about 4 minutes.

Spoon a ¼-inch layer of the cooked pinto beans in the bottom of each cassolette. Arrange 3 or 4 sweetbread pieces in a circle on top, and place 1 tablespoon of the cooked wild rice in the center. Serve immediately.

Quenelles of Turkey with a Sauce of Chickpeas and Pineapple

Quenelles are an ethereal dish. Made light with beaten egg and cream, they puff up when poached, almost doubling in size. These turkey quenelles include small dice of ham, which punctuate the mild mousse with their smoky flavor. The sauce combines similar contrasts—chickpeas, with their mild nutlike flavor, and the sharp tropical taste of fresh pineapple.

TO SERVE 6

For the Chickpea Sauce: Put the chickpeas, ham, garlic, onion and water in a medium saucepan. Bring to a boil over moderate-to-high heat, then reduce the heat and simmer, covered, until the chickpeas are tender and about ¾ cup of cooking liquid remains, about 1 hour.

While the chickpeas are cooking, put the cream into a small saucepan over moderate-to-high heat. Bring it to a boil, reduce the heat and cook it at a low rolling boil until it reduces to 1½ cups, about 10 minutes.

Put the chickpeas, their cooking liquid and the cream in a processor. Process until finely pureed, then pass the puree through a sieve, return it to the pan and set it aside.

For the Turkey Quenelles: Put the turkey breast cubes in a processor with the cream, salt and pepper. Process until finely pureed, then pulse in the egg and the Madeira. Remove the puree from the processor into a mixing bowl and fold in the ham.

Bring the chicken stock to a boil in a medium saucepan. Reduce the heat to maintain a bare simmer. Mold the quenelle mixture between the bowls of 2 wet tablespoons, dropping the quenelles carefully into the stock. Poach for 2 minutes per side, turning them gently and basting their tops continuously with the stock. Remove the quenelles with a slotted spoon and drain them on paper towels.

Put the pan of sauce back over moderate heat to warm gently. In a separate pan, melt the butter in a small skillet and sauté the pineapple cubes for about 2 minutes to warm them through.

Spoon the sauce in a circle in the center of each large warmed serving plate. Sprinkle pineapple cubes over the sauce and place 2 quenelles side by side in the center.

◥ Chickpea Sauce and Pineapple
½ cup dried chickpeas, soaked overnight
1 small ham hock
2 whole garlic cloves, peeled
½ a small onion, coarsely chopped
3 cups water
2 cups heavy cream
1 tablespoon unsalted butter

◥ Turkey Quenelles
1 pound boned raw skinless turkey breast, trimmed and cut into 1-inch pieces
1 cup heavy cream
1 teaspoon salt
1 teaspoon white pepper
1 egg
1 tablespoon Madeira
½ pound good-quality cooked ham, cut into ¼-inch cubes
4 cups Chicken Stock (page 211)

1 small fresh pineapple, peeled, cored and cut into ¼-inch cubes

Top: *Red Chile Relleno with Lobster and Coulis of Green Tomato and Cilantro.* Bottom, left: *Green Chile Relleno with Duxelles and Garlic Chèvre Sauce.* Bottom, right: *Zebra of Red and Green Chile Relleno with Lobster Sauce*

Green Chiles Rellenos with Duxelles and Garlic Chèvre Sauce

This has become a sort of signature dish at Saint Estèphe. Every reviewer mentions it, and every magazine article and newspaper feature seems to show a picture of it. Really the recipe is very simple: a few spoons of *duxelles*, the classic French mushroom reduction, stuffed inside a roasted mild green chile, served on top of an easily made sauce of goat cheese and garlic, then decorated with a few lines of Red Chile Indian Paint. I think it is this very simplicity that's so appealing.

TO SERVE 6

For the Duxelles: Melt the butter in a large saucepan over moderate heat. Add the mushrooms and sauté them until all their liquid evaporates, about 20 minutes. Stir in the cream, salt and pepper. Continue cooking the mushrooms, stirring occasionally, until they have absorbed all the cream and the mixture is thick, about 20 minutes more. Set the Duxelles aside to cool.

For the Garlic Chèvre Sauce: Put the wine, garlic and salt in a medium saucepan over moderate-to-high heat and boil until reduced by half, about 5 minutes. Stir in the cream and goat cheese with a wire whisk, then pass the sauce through a sieve. Set it aside and keep warm.

While the sauce is cooking, spread the chiles open on the work surface. Lightly salt their insides and spoon 3 tablespoons of the Duxelles along the length of each. Fold the chiles closed and place them, seam side down, on a buttered baking sheet. Preheat the oven to 425°F.

When the sauce is ready, cover the rellenos with a damp kitchen towel and bake them until heated through, about 10 minutes.

Put the Red Chile Indian Paint into a plastic squeeze bottle. Spoon the sauce into the middle of each large warmed serving plate. Place a chile along one side of each plate. With the squeeze bottle, paint a pair of zigzags, or another design of your choice, on the other side of each plate.

◤ Duxelles
1 tablespoon unsalted butter
2 pounds button mushrooms, washed, dried and finely chopped
½ cup heavy cream
½ teaspoon salt
½ teaspoon white pepper

◤ Garlic Chèvre Sauce
½ cup dry white wine
3 garlic cloves, finely chopped
½ teaspoon salt
2 cups heavy cream
5 ounces aged creamy goat cheese

6 fresh green Anaheim chiles, roasted, skinned and seeded (page 22)
½ teaspoon salt
¼ cup Red Chile Indian Paint (page 209)

Red Chiles Rellenos with Lobster and Coulis of Green Tomato and Cilantro

We normally think of using green chiles for chiles rellenos. But in the Fall, Anaheim chiles ripened for an extra-long time turn red, and they make beautiful rellenos. The roasted red chiles have a wonderful sweetness that I think goes very well with lobster. A bright green, thick puree—what the French call a *coulis*—of green tomatoes and cilantro adds color to the presentation and a sharp contrast to the flavors of lobster and roasted pepper. Since it is also sometimes necessary to pick green tomatoes in fall to save them from early frost, this is a lovely end-of-summer dish.

TO SERVE 6

Red Chiles Rellenos with Lobster

3 small lobsters, about 1 pound each, boiled for 10 minutes and cooled
1 quart water
1 teaspoon kosher salt
3 mushrooms, cut into ⅛-inch dice
1 very small carrot, cut into ⅛-inch dice
1 very small onion, cut into ⅛-inch dice
1 small celery stalk, cut into ⅛-inch dice
6 fresh red Anaheim chiles, roasted, skinned and seeded (page 22)
1 teaspoon salt
1 teaspoon white pepper

Coulis of Green Tomato and Cilantro

1 tablespoon olive oil
1 medium garlic clove, finely chopped
1 medium shallot, finely chopped

For the Red Chiles Rellenos of Lobster: Crack open the lobsters and remove their tail meat; cut the meat into fine shreds. Remove the soft, bright yellow liver and combine it with the shredded tail meat in a mixing bowl. Crack and peel the claws, keeping them whole, and set them aside.

Bring 1 quart of water to a boil with 1 teaspoon of kosher salt in a small saucepan. Add the mushrooms, carrot, onion and celery and blanch them for 10 seconds; drain them well.

Add the vegetables to the shredded lobster and liver and mix them well. Season the insides of the chiles with salt and white pepper. Spoon the mixture into the chiles, and then fold them closed. Place the chiles seam side down on a buttered baking sheet and set aside.

For the Coulis: Heat the olive oil in a medium saucepan over moderate heat. Add the garlic and shallot and sauté them for about 3 minutes, then add the green tomatoes and wine. Cook the mixture, stirring occasionally, for about 10 minutes. Then stir in the cilantro and continue cooking until thick, about 10 minutes more.

While the tomatoes are cooking, preheat the oven to 425°F. Cover the rellenos with a damp kitchen towel and bake them until heated through, about 10 minutes.

Sieve the coulis and spoon it into the center of each large, heated serving plate. Place a relleno on top of the sauce and a lobster claw beside it.

10 large green tomatoes (*not* tomatillos), peeled, seeded and coarsely chopped
1 cup dry white wine
2 tablespoons chopped fresh cilantro

Zebra of Red and Green Chiles Rellenos with Lobster Sauce

I created this dish initially to serve at "The Cutting Edge," a November 1985 dinner featuring fourteen Los Angeles chefs and twelve Southern California wineries to launch the Los Angeles chapter of the American Institute of Wine and Food. The version served that night was stuffed completely with mushroom duxelles, and served with the garlic chèvre sauce that accompanies my green chile relleno; it was accompanied by a Firestone Cabernet Sauvignon. In this version of the recipe, the red and green chiles have two different stuffings, and the zebras are served with a rich lobster sauce.

With the help of the other chefs and their kitchen staffs, the zebras were served to 500 guests. It was a difficult challenge. But my colleagues did an admirable job in heating the huge trays of rellenos, transferring them to sauced serving plates, painting the plates and sending them off in the hands of dozens of waiters—all in less than four minutes. Unless you have a huge kitchen, and a staff to match, I wouldn't recommend serving this dish to more than six, or maybe twelve, people at a time.

Start to prepare the zebras by assembling three each of the Red Chiles Rellenos with Lobster and the Green Chiles Rellenos with Duxelles (see recipes above); they are then sliced and reassembled into "zebras" before heating. Save the top part of the lobster bodies and the legs when you make the Red Chiles Rellenos filling; they will be used to flavor the sauce.

TO SERVE 6

▼ *Zebras of Red and Green Chiles Rellenos*

3 red Chiles Rellenos with Lobster (page 90), uncooked
3 Green Chiles Rellenos with Duxelles (page 89), uncooked

▼ *Lobster Sauce*

Lobster bodies and legs, without heads, reserved from Red Chiles Rellenos filling
2 cups Fish Stock (page 211)
2 cups dry white wine
¼ cup tomato paste
2 medium carrots, coarsely chopped
1 medium onion, coarsely chopped
3 tablespoons coarsely chopped fresh tarragon, or 1 tablespoon dried
1 tablespoon coarsely chopped fresh thyme, or 1 teaspoon dried
1 bunch parsley, leaves only
1 bay leaf
1 cup heavy cream
½ teaspoon salt
½ teaspoon white pepper

¼ cup Red Chile Indian Paint (page 209), at room temperature

For the Zebras of Red and Green Chiles Rellenos: Place the prepared rellenos on a work surface and, with a sharp knife, carefully cut each relleno diagonally into 6 neat equal pieces. On a buttered baking tray, carefully reassemble the chiles, alternating red and green pieces, to make 6 zebra-striped rellenos. Set them aside.

For the Lobster Sauce: Put the lobster shells in a processor and pulse to crush them into small ¼-to-½-inch pieces. Put the crushed shells in a medium saucepan with the stock, wine, tomato paste, carrots, onion and herbs. Bring the liquid to a boil over moderate-to-high heat, stirring occasionally; adjust the heat to maintain a low rolling boil and continue cooking until the liquid has reduced to 1 cup, about 35 minutes.

While the lobster liquid is reducing, bring the cream to a boil in a small saucepan over moderate-to-high heat; reduce it at a low rolling boil to ½ cup, about 10 minutes.

Preheat the oven to 425°F. Cover the rellenos with a damp kitchen towel and bake them until heated through, about 10 minutes.

Pass the lobster shell mixture through a coarse sieve to remove the vegetables, herbs and shell particles. Stir the reduced cream and seasonings into the lobster liquid and pass the sauce through a fine sieve. Return the sauce to the pan and warm it gently over moderate heat, about 2 minutes; do not boil.

Spoon the sauce into the middle of each large warmed serving plate. With a spatula, carefully transfer a zebra of rellenos to one side of each plate. Put the Red Indian Paint into a plastic squeeze bottle and paint a pair of zigzags, or another design of your choice, on the other side of each plate.

Green Chile Soufflé

In France, the making of a soufflé was the ultimate test of a chef's skill, just as Venetian artists centuries ago were judged by their ability to paint a perfect egg. I've given a fiery Southwestern touch to the soufflé's classic elegance with the addition of jalapeño chiles.

TO SERVE 6

Preheat the oven to 400°F.

In a medium saucepan, melt 4 tablespoons of the butter over moderate heat. Stir in 4 tablespoons of the flour and cook for 2 minutes, or until nutty brown but not burned. Stir in the milk, whisking continuously, until well incorporated and pasty, about 2 minutes.

Remove the pan from the heat and thoroughly stir in the egg yolks, 2 at a time. Then stir in the goat cheese, red bell pepper, jalapeños and seasonings.

Beat the egg whites until they form stiff peaks. Gently fold them into the goat cheese and chile mixture.

Prepare 6 4-ounce soufflé dishes by coating their bottoms and sides with the remaining butter and flour, then molding collars of aluminum foil around them extending 1 inch above their rims. Carefully spoon the soufflé mixture into the prepared dishes. Bake the soufflés for about 18 minutes, or until firm to the touch and golden.

7 tablespoons unsalted butter
7 tablespoons all-purpose flour
1½ cups milk, scalded
6 eggs, separated, at room temperature
4 ounces aged creamy goat cheese
1 tablespoon finely chopped roasted red bell pepper (page 22)
1 teaspoon finely chopped roasted jalapeño chiles (page 22)
½ teaspoon salt
½ teaspoon white pepper

Scrambled Huevos Rancheros with Blue Corn Tortilla Arrows

Huevos Rancheros is Spanish for "ranch-style eggs," and in Southwestern cooking it usually means a fried corn tortilla topped with a layer of refried beans, a couple of eggs fried in lard or butter, shredded jack cheese and lots of hot chile salsa.

I wanted to keep the ethnic connection of the chiles and the tortillas in these Huevos Rancheros, yet turn out a much lighter dish. In this version, I scramble the eggs with jalapeños and goat cheese and serve them in their shells, garnished with arrowhead-shaped strips of blue corn tortillas. (See page 98 for another version of Huevos Rancheros.)

TO SERVE 6

▼▫ *Blue Corn Tortilla Arrows*
3 blue corn tortillas
  Vegetable oil for frying

▼▫ *Scrambled Huevos Rancheros*
12 eggs
2 tablespoons unsalted butter
6 tablespoons finely diced white onion
3 teaspoons diced roasted jalapeño chiles (page 22)
5 teaspoons diced roasted red bell peppers (page 22)
4 ounces aged creamy goat cheese, coarsely chopped
¼ cup half-and-half

For the Tortilla Arrows: Cut each tortilla into 12 arrowheads (as shown on opposite page). Heat ½ inch of oil in a large heavy skillet over high heat to 375°F. on a deep-frying thermometer and fry the arrowheads in several batches until crisp, about 2 minutes per batch. Drain them on paper towels and pat off any excess oil.

For the Scrambled Huevos Rancheros: Use an egg cutter to carefully cut off the top quarter of the narrow end of each egg. Empty the eggs into a bowl and carefully rinse out and dry the insides of the shells. Beat the eggs.

Melt the butter in a saucepan over moderate heat and sauté the onion until very lightly golden, about 1 minute. Lower the heat and add the beaten eggs and the remaining ingredients and cook, stirring frequently, for only about 3 minutes—the eggs should still be very creamy.

Carefully spoon the scrambled eggs into the eggshells, mounding them slightly, and place each shell in an egg cup. Stand 3 tortilla arrows around 1 side of the inside rim of each eggshell and serve immediately.

Scrambled Huevos Rancheros with Blue Corn Tortilla Arrows

CHAPTER 4

SALADS

Salad of Huevos Rancheros with Poached Eggs and Spaghetti of Cucumber

Salad of Huevos Rancheros with Poached Eggs and Spaghetti of Cucumber

Here's another of my variations on the Southwestern concept of *Huevos Rancheros* (page 94). In this dish the principal elements become a light salad, served in a "nest" made from tortilla strips and a spaghettilike julienne of cucumber, dressed with a spicy jalapeño vinaigrette.

TO SERVE 6

Jalapeño Vinaigrette
¼ cup sherry vinegar
1 teaspoon pepper
¾ teaspoon salt
¾ cup walnut oil
1 teaspoon diced roasted jalapeño chiles (page 22)
1 teaspoon diced roasted red bell peppers (page 22)

Vegetable oil for frying
3 blue corn tortillas, cut into ⅛-inch strips
3 gold corn tortillas, cut into ⅛-inch strips
2 medium cucumbers, peeled, halved lengthwise and seeded
12 eggs

For the Jalapeño Vinaigrette: Stir together the vinegar, pepper and salt. Stir in the oil, then the jalapeños and red bell peppers.

Heat ½ inch of vegetable oil in a large heavy skillet over high heat to 375°F. on a deep-frying thermometer. Fry the tortilla strips in several batches for 15 seconds each, until tender but not crisp. Drain them on paper towels, patting off excess oil, and put them in a mixing bowl.

With a mandoline or a large, sharp knife, cut the cucumber lengthwise into long, thin julienne strips that resemble strands of spaghetti. Put them in the bowl with the tortilla strips and toss them together with ¼ cup of the Jalapeño Vinaigrette.

Fill a shallow saucepan two-thirds full of water and bring it to a boil. Reduce the heat to the barest simmer and carefully break the eggs into the water. Poach the eggs, 4 at a time, for about 3 minutes, until the whites are firm but the yolks still liquid. Carefully remove the eggs with a slotted spoon and drain well on paper towels.

Arrange the tortilla-cucumber mixture on serving plates in the shape of a bird's nest. Place a pair of poached eggs in the center of each nest. Serve at once.

Salad of Red Cabbage and Roquefort with Hot Bacon Vinaigrette and Sage Crouton Arrows

This is the last lingering, purely French dish from the original menu at Saint Estèphe. It's such a classic combination, and so good, that it continues to be one of our most popular salad courses. I *have* given it one new Southwestern touch: crisp croutons, cut in the shape of arrowheads and flavored with sage, a common herb in New Mexico.

TO SERVE 6

For the Salad of Red Cabbage and Roquefort: Bring 4 quarts of water with 2 tablespoons of kosher salt to a boil in a large saucepan. Add the cabbage shreds and blanch them for 30 seconds, then drain well and let the cabbage cool to room temperature. Toss the cabbage together with the cheese in a large salad bowl.

For the Sage Crouton Arrows: Preheat the oven to 325°F. With a small, sharp knife, cut each slice of bread into 3 arrowhead shapes. Brush both sides of the arrowheads with the butter and place them on a baking sheet. Sprinkle them evenly with the sage, pressing it into the bread. Bake the croutons for about 12 minutes, then turn them over and cook for 4 minutes more, until they are evenly golden brown.

For the Hot Bacon Vinaigrette: Stir together the vinegar, salt and pepper until the salt dissolves. Stir in the mustard, then the oil. Sauté the bacon in a medium skillet over low-to-moderate heat just until cooked through but not yet crisp, about 3 minutes. Pour off the fat, add the dressing to the skillet, and let it warm for 1 to 2 minutes. Pour the warm dressing over the cabbage and Roquefort and toss the salad well. Mound the salad on the top half of each large serving plate. Place a pair of croutons on the bottom half, pointing toward the salad.

☞ **Salad of Red Cabbage and Roquefort**
- 1 medium head red cabbage, cored, quartered and cut into ⅛-inch shreds
- 2 tablespoons kosher salt
- 6 ounces Roquefort cheese, crumbled

☞ **Sage Crouton Arrows**
- 4 slices dense egg bread, such as brioche or pullman, crusts trimmed
- 4 tablespoons unsalted butter, softened
- 1 teaspoon salt
- 1 teaspoon white pepper
- 20 fresh sage leaves, very finely chopped, or 2 teaspoons dried sage

☞ **Hot Bacon Vinaigrette**
- 3 tablespoons red wine vinegar
- 1 teaspoon salt
- 2 teaspoons black pepper
- 2 tablespoons hot Dijon mustard
- 12 tablespoons vegetable oil
- 6 ounces smoked bacon, cut into ¼-inch cubes

Avocado Cake with Blue and Gold Tortilla Arrows

This recipe transforms the familiar casual party dish known as guacamole into an elegant appetizer.

TO SERVE 6

≡≡≡

3 small tomatoes
3 ears of corn, shucked, strings removed
3 ripe medium-size avocados
5 garlic cloves, coarsely chopped
Juice of 1 lemon
1½ teaspoons salt
1½ teaspoons white pepper
Blue and gold corn tortilla chips (page 197)

Bring a saucepan of salted water to a boil. Cut out the stem end of the tomatoes and, using a very sharp knife, cut an "X" in the skin on their bottoms. Blanch them in the boiling water for just 30 seconds. Remove and set aside. When cool enough to handle, peel the tomatoes, halve them and spoon out their seeds. Cut the flesh into ⅛-inch dice and set aside.

Bring another saucepan of salted water to a boil. With a serrated knife, cut the kernels from the ears of corn. Cook them in the water for 3 minutes, then drain well and set them aside.

Peel and seed the avocado and put it in the processor with the garlic, lemon juice and seasonings. Process to a smooth, creamy puree.

To assemble the avocado cake, place an 11-inch circular bottomless ring mold (about 1 inch high) in the center of a large serving platter. Spread the cooked corn in a thin layer inside the ring. Place a thin layer of diced tomato on top. Fill the mold to the top with the avocado puree, and use a narrow spatula or a long knife to smooth the puree level with the rim of the mold. Lift off the mold and surround the avocado cake with a mixture of blue and gold corn tortilla chips.

Avocado Cake with Blue and Gold Tortilla Arrows

Desert Salad of Duck Jerky, Melon, Pumpkin Seeds and Lamb's-Quarters

In the old Southwest, meat was "jerked"—seasoned and sun-dried—to preserve it for the long winter months when no fresh meat was available. Today, jerky is appreciated not so much as a practical staple as it is for its strong, spicy flavor and crisp yet chewy texture.

At Saint Estèphe we make a jerky from duck—which has a strong enough flavor to stand up to the spices—and serve it in a salad based on lamb's-quarters. This mild, elegant salad green, also known as mâche or corn salad, grows wild in the high plateau deserts of New Mexico after thunderstorms. Commercially raised lamb's-quarters are available in gourmet supermarkets; if you can't find it, substitute *verdolagas* (page 133), wild spinach, or a very tender, mild lettuce such as butter or salad bowl.

TO SERVE 6

⧉⤳ Duck Jerky
2 large meaty duck breasts (Mulard or Muscovy), about 6 ounces each, skinned and boned
2 teaspoons chile pequín (available in Latin markets)
½ tablespoon kosher salt
1 teaspoon coarsely ground black pepper
1 tablespoon vegetable oil
1 small garlic clove, finely chopped

For the Duck Jerky: With a sharp knife, slice the duck breasts almost parallel to the work surface into long slices as thin as possible. Line a large baking sheet with waxed paper. Place the duck slices in a medium-size bowl and season with the chile, salt and pepper. Then combine the oil and garlic and rub it all over the slices. Place the slices on the lined baking sheet in a single layer, without overlapping. Cover them with another sheet of waxed paper and put them in the refrigerator to marinate overnight.

The next day, dehydrate the duck slices. Use a home food dehydrater or smoker, if possible, following the manufacturer's instructions. Otherwise, place the duck slices in a single layer on a wire rack, so air circulates around them. If using a gas stove, put the sheets in the turned-off oven, using only the heat from the pilot light. For an electric stove, set the oven at its lowest possible temperature: if it is as low as 100°F., leave the door closed; if the lowest setting is higher, leave the door slightly ajar. Dry the duck until the slices are very dry but still slightly flexible and tender, 4 to 6 hours. (The duck jerky may be stored in an airtight container in a dry place for up to 5 days.)

For the Dressing: Stir together the vinegar, salt and pepper until the salt dissolves. Stir in the oregano leaves, then gradually stir in the olive oil. Set the dressing aside.

For the Desert Salad: Place each cantaloupe half cut side down on the work surface and cut it vertically into ¼-inch slices. Then cut each slice parallel to its flat edge into ¼-inch-thick pieces.

Toss the melon pieces, lamb's-quarters and pumpkins seeds with the dressing. Arrange the salad on each chilled serving plate. With your fingers, shred the duck jerky and sprinkle it generously on top.

Dressing
⅛ cup red wine vinegar
½ teaspoon salt
½ teaspoon black pepper
 1 teaspoon fresh oregano leaves, washed and patted dry
½ cup light olive oil

 1 medium cantaloupe, halved, seeded and peeled
30 clusters lamb's-quarters, leaves separated, washed and dried (about 3 cups total)
½ cup shelled pumpkin seeds, toasted (page 24)

Marinated Fresh Hearts of Palm with Zucchini Salsa

The public's demand in recent years for unusual new foods has made available an incredible variety of fresh foods from around the world. Until recently, hearts of palm could only be found canned in a marinade or brine; now you can sometimes find them fresh in good vegetable markets.

Fresh hearts of palm come encased in sections of tough stalk, which have to be cut open carefully with a large, sharp knife to expose the vegetable within. The hearts have a wonderfully delicate flavor that, I find, goes well with a subtle dressing such as the Zucchini Salsa in this recipe. If you can't find fresh hearts of palm, use a good-quality canned variety.

TO SERVE 6

☞ *Marinated Fresh Hearts of Palm*

1 large (12-inch) section of hearts of palm, tough outer bark slit open and peeled off to reveal the hearts (or quartered canned hearts of palm)

1 tablespoon Jalapeño Vinegar (page 203)

½ medium garlic clove, finely chopped

¼ teaspoon salt

¼ teaspoon black pepper

3 tablespoons vegetable oil

☞ *Zucchini Salsa*

1 tablespoon Jalapeño Vinegar (page 203)

½ medium garlic clove, finely chopped

¼ teaspoon salt

¼ teaspoon black pepper

3 tablespoons vegetable oil

1 medium zucchini, split lengthwise, seeded and finely chopped

1 medium tomato, peeled, seeded and finely chopped

½ small onion, finely chopped

12 small sprigs cilantro, for garnish

For the Marinated Fresh Hearts of Palm: Cut the hearts of palm in half. Separate them into sections and cut the sections into a total of 48 sticks (or use enough quartered canned hearts to make 48 sticks).

In a medium-size mixing bowl, stir together the vinegar, garlic, salt and pepper until the salt dissolves. Vigorously stir in the oil. Toss the hearts of palm with this marinade, cover the bowl, and leave the hearts in the refrigerator to marinate for about 1 hour.

For the Zucchini Salsa: Stir together the vinegar, garlic, salt and pepper until the salt dissolves. Vigorously stir in the oil, then stir in the zucchini, tomato and onion.

Spoon the salsa into the centers of 6 large chilled serving plates. Stack 8 sticks of hearts of palm on each plate: place 2 parallel sticks on a slant, 2 more parallel sticks crossing the first 2, then 2 more pairs of sticks crossing on top. Garnish each plate with 2 sprigs of cilantro.

Marinated Fresh Hearts of Palm with Zucchini Salsa

Radicchio Tacos with Smoked Chicken, Asparagus and Red Chile Mayonnaise

This is salad as finger food with radicchio leaves taking the place of a tortilla shell to make a kind of taco.

TO SERVE 6

2 teaspoons kosher salt
12 fresh asparagus spears, stems peeled
12 ounces smoked chicken (available at gourmet shops), skinned, boned and coarsely shredded

◼◻ Red Chile Mayonnaise
1 egg yolk
1 tablespoon mustard
¼ teaspoon salt
¼ teaspoon white pepper
1 teaspoon red wine vinegar
½ cup salad oil
3 teaspoons diced pimentos
½ teaspoon diced roasted jalapeño chiles (page 22)

12 radicchio leaves
12 whole chives, dipped in hot water to wilt

Bring 2 quarts of water to a boil with 2 teaspoons of kosher salt in a large saucepan. Tie the asparagus in a bundle with kitchen string and stand it, tips up, in the water. Simmer, covered, for 8 minutes, until tender but still firm. Transfer the asparagus to a bowl of ice water to stop the cooking. When cool, trim each spear to leave a 2-inch tip section; reserve the stems for another recipe.

For the Red Chile Mayonnaise: Put the yolk, mustard, salt, pepper and half of the vinegar in a food processor and process until thick and lemon-yellow in color. With the motor running, very slowly add the oil. When all the oil has been added and the mayonnaise is thick, process in the rest of the vinegar and the pimentos and jalapeños.

For the Radicchio Tacos: Combine the smoked chicken shreds with 5 tablespoons of the mayonnaise. Spread open each radicchio leaf and spoon the chicken mixture inside; top with an asparagus tip. Close each leaf and tie it tightly with a chive.

Mosaic of Vegetables Navajo-Style with Garlic Mayonnaise

Every time I go home to Santa Fe, I see Navajos in the Plaza wearing brightly colored blankets with large geometric patterns. Native jewelers also spread these blankets on the ground in the Plaza as a backdrop for their intricate jewelry worked in turquoise and silver. This salad arrangement, in color and design, is inspired by those vivid Navajo blankets.

TO SERVE 6

For the Mosaic of Vegetables: Trim the carrots, turnip and beet into long 4-sided wedges, with sides 1 inch long, that in cross-section resemble diamond shapes. Cut each wedge crosswise into thin slices, ⅛ to ¼ inch thick, to make a total of 30 diamonds of carrot, 48 of turnip and 60 of beet. Cut each green bean in half lengthwise, and then cut the halves into 1-inch pieces to make 48 pieces in all.

Bring 2 quarts of water to a boil in a large saucepan with 2 teaspoons of kosher salt. Prepare 4 separate bowls of ice water. Blanch the vegetable diamonds in the boiling water in separate batches, removing each with a slotted spoon or wire skimmer and immediately plunging it into ice water: boil the turnips first for 45 seconds, then the beans for 1 minute, the carrots for 2 minutes and the beets for 3 minutes.

Remove the vegetables from their bowls and pat dry, keeping them separate. Place a row of 5 carrot diamonds side by side across the center of each large chilled serving plate. Place a row of 4 turnip diamonds interlocking above and below each row of carrots. Place a row of 5 beet diamonds interlocking at the top and bottom of each mosaic. At the top, bottom and each side of the plate, place an "X" of 2 green bean pieces. Chill the plates in the refrigerator while you prepare the mayonnaise.

For the Garlic Mayonnaise: Beat the egg yolks with the vinegar, mustard, salt and pepper until light and creamy. Then, whisking continuously, slowly add the olive oil, increasing the flow slightly as the mayonnaise begins to thicken to a light, smooth consistency. Stir in the chopped garlic. The mayonnaise can also be prepared in a food processor. To do this, put the yolks, half the

≣⊃ Mosaic of Vegetables
2 large carrots, peeled
1 large turnip, peeled
1 large raw beet, peeled
6 large green beans, trimmed
2 teaspoons kosher salt

≣⊃ Garlic Mayonnaise
3 egg yolks, at room temperature
1 tablespoon red wine vinegar
½ teaspoon Dijon mustard
½ teaspoon salt
½ teaspoon white pepper
½ cup light olive oil
2 small garlic cloves, finely chopped

vinegar, mustard, salt and pepper in a food processor and process until thick. With the motor running, very slowly add the oil. When all the oil has been added and the mayonnaise is thick, process in the rest of the vinegar and the garlic. Serve the mayonnaise alongside the chilled mosaics.

Duck Chicharrones Salad with Dijon Mustard Vinaigrette

Crisp-fried pork cracklings, vividly named *chicharrones* are a favorite Southwestern snack. I like to make cracklings of duck, which have a much richer, more complex flavor, and serve them in an elegant salad with watercress, jicama and a Dijon mustard vinaigrette.

For these Duck Chicharrones, you will need the fat and skin from the neck and tail ends of two ducks. Reserve them from another recipe (they will keep well in the freezer), or ask your butcher to reserve them for you.

TO SERVE 6

For the Duck Chicharrones Salad: Season the duck fat and skin with the salt and pepper. Heat the oil in a large skillet over moderate heat. Lay the pieces of duck fat and skin flat in the skillet; place a smaller skillet or heavy saucepan inside the skillet to hold the pieces flat.

Reduce the heat to moderate-to-low and cook, turning them 3 or 4 times, until all the duck fat is rendered and the skins are very crisp and brown, about 20 minutes. Remove the cracklings and pat them dry with paper towels. Cut them into ¼-inch strips. Toss them together with the watercress leaves and jícama.

For the Dijon Mustard Vinaigrette: Stir together the vinegar, pepper and salt until the salt dissolves, then stir in the mustard. Pouring the oil in a slow stream, whisk it into the vinegar-mustard mixture until well incorporated.

Toss the salad ingredients together with the dressing. Serve the salad on chilled serving plates.

Mosaic of Vegetables Navajo-Style with Garlic Mayonnaise

☞ Duck Chicharrones Salad
Neck and tail fat and skin from 2 ducks, in large neat pieces
1 teaspoon salt
1 teaspoon black pepper
2 tablespoons vegetable oil
3 bunches watercress, stemmed, washed and dried
1 small (or ½ large) jícama, peeled and cut into ⅛-inch strips

☞ Dijon Mustard Vinaigrette
2 tablespoons red wine vinegar
1 teaspoon black pepper
½ teaspoon salt
2 tablespoons extra-strong Dijon mustard
5 tablespoons vegetable oil

Orange, Nopal and Lamb Salad with Red Chile Vinaigrette

Lamb and citrus go well with the fresh green taste of nopal cactus, and all of their flavors are sparked by the dried chile in the dressing. The dressing calls for oregano-flavored red wine vinegar, which you can buy in many gourmet food stores; or make your own by leaving three sprigs of fresh oregano in a bottle of vinegar for at least a week. This recipe is sufficient for a main-course luncheon dish for 4.

TO SERVE 6 AS AN APPETIZER

⬛☞ Orange, Nopal and Lamb Salad

4 large navel oranges
2 tablespoons kosher salt
2 large nopal cactus pads, scraped and trimmed (page 24) and cut into 2-inch by ¼-inch pieces
2 whole lamb fillets, about 6 ounces each
¼ teaspoon salt
¼ teaspoon black pepper
1 tablespoon vegetable oil
6 large nopal cactus pads, scraped and trimmed, for garnish

⬛☞ Red Chile Vinaigrette

2 tablespoons oregano red wine vinegar
1 tablespoon finely chopped dried red Chimayo chile
½ teaspoon salt
½ teaspoon black pepper
6 tablespoons vegetable oil

For the Orange, Nopal and Lamb Salad: With a small, sharp knife, thickly peel the oranges, cutting away all pith and outer membrane as well. Cut between the inner membranes to separate the oranges into segments, totally free from all membranes. Put the segments in a mixing bowl.

Bring 2 quarts of water with 2 tablespoons of kosher salt to a rolling boil in a medium saucepan. Add the cactus pieces to the water and, as soon as the water returns to a boil and the cactus turns a lime-green color—after about 30 seconds—drain them in a strainer. Hold the strainer under cold running water and continue rinsing the cactus pieces, tossing them with your fingers, until no more syruplike gum runs out of the strainer with the water and the cactus pieces no longer feel gummy to the touch. Drain well and add the cactus to the orange segments.

Season the lamb fillets with salt and pepper. Heat the oil in a medium skillet over moderate-to-high heat until very hot and sear the lamb fillets on all 4 sides until medium-rare, about 45 seconds per side. Remove the fillets and pat them with paper towels. With a sharp knife, cut each fillet diagonally into 9 slices. Add the slices to the oranges and cactus.

For the Red Chile Vinaigrette: Stir together the vinegar, chile, salt and pepper until the salt dissolves. Pouring the oil in a slow stream, whisk it into the vinegar until well incorporated.

Add the dressing to the oranges, cactus and lamb and gently toss the salad. Arrange it on serving plates, making sure that each serving gets 3 slices of lamb. Garnish each plate with a whole nopal cactus pad.

Orange, Nopal and Lamb Salad with Red Chile Vinaigrette

Cactus-Corn Cactus Salad with Smoked Mussels and Mustard Seed Vinaigrette

In this playful presentation, fresh corn kernels and corn-sized dice of nopal cactus are tossed with a thick Pommery mustard dressing; they are then arranged in the shape of a saguaro cactus, the Southwestern species that often humorously seems to mimic human forms. Rich, meaty smoked mussels, widely available in cans or jars from gourmet stores, add a striking contrast to the sharp flavors and crisp textures of the vegetables.

TO SERVE 6

1 teaspoon kosher salt
3 medium ears of corn, shucked, strings removed, kernels cut from cobs (about 1½ cups)
2 8-inch nopal cactus pads, scraped and trimmed (page 24) and cut into ¼-inch dice (about 1½ cups)

Mustard Seed Vinaigrette
3 teaspoons red wine vinegar
⅛ teaspoon salt
⅛ teaspoon white pepper
4 teaspoons Pommery mustard
2 tablespoons vegetable oil
2 teaspoons finely chopped fresh tarragon

36 small smoked mussels
6 small sprigs of fresh tarragon

Bring 2 quarts of water with 1 teaspoon of kosher salt to a rolling boil in a medium saucepan. Add the corn kernels and boil them for about 3 minutes, until tender. Strain them through a colander, retaining the water and returning it to the pan.

Bring the water back to a boil and add the cactus pieces. As soon as the water returns to a boil and the cactus turns a lime-green color—after about 30 seconds—drain them in a strainer. Hold the strainer under cold running water and continue rinsing the cactus pieces, tossing them with your fingers, until no more syruplike gum runs out of the strainer with the water and the cactus pieces no longer feel gummy to the touch.

For the Mustard Vinaigrette: Stir together the vinegar, salt and pepper until the salt dissolves, then stir in the mustard. Pouring the oil in a slow stream, whisk it into the vinegar-mustard mixture until well incorporated, then stir in the tarragon.

Toss the corn and cactus together with about 4 tablespoons of the dressing. With a spoon, arrange the mixture on the left-hand side of each large chilled serving plate in the form of a saguaro cactus; use 4 or 5 tablespoons to form the long trunk of the cactus, and another 1½ tablespoons or so to form each upward-curving armlike branch, 1 on each side of the trunk (see photograph on opposite page).

Toss the mussels with the remaining dressing, coating them lightly. Cluster 6 mussels in the center of the right-hand side of each plate, and decorate them with a sprig of tarragon.

Cactus-Corn Cactus Salad with Smoked Mussels and Mustard Seed Vinaigrette

Spaghetti of Cucumber and Salmon with Pasta in Cilantro Mayonnaise

This elegant salad gets a hint of Southwestern flavor from a whole bunch of cilantro leaves mixed into its mayonnaise dressing.

TO SERVE 6

⊒⫐ Spaghetti of Cucumber and Salmon with Pasta

4 medium cucumbers, peeled and halved lengthwise
½ pound Egg Pasta (page 201)
2 tablespoons kosher salt
4 tablespoons vegetable oil
6 ounces thinly sliced smoked salmon

⊒⫐ Cilantro Mayonnaise

½ cup Basic Mayonnaise (page 208)
1 bunch cilantro, leaves only
1 tablespoon red wine vinegar
½ teaspoon salt
½ teaspoon white pepper

For the Spaghetti of Cucumber and Salmon with Pasta: With a mandoline or a food processor fitted with a julienne disk, cut the cucumbers lengthwise into long, thin spaghettilike strands. Put the strands in a sieve to drain.

Roll out the pasta dough as thinly as possible and cut it into very thin "angel hair" spaghetti strands. In a large saucepan, bring 2 quarts of water to a full, rolling boil with 2 tablespoons of kosher salt and 2 tablespoons of vegetable oil. Cook the pasta until tender but still slightly chewy (al dente), about 4 minutes. Drain the pasta and toss it with 2 tablespoons of vegetable oil.

Cut the smoked salmon slices into long, thin strands. Toss the salmon, cucumber and pasta together in a mixing bowl.

For the Cilantro Mayonnaise: Stir together the mayonnaise, cilantro, vinegar, salt and pepper.

Gently toss the salad ingredients with the dressing. Chill the salad in the refrigerator for at least 1 hour. Serve it on chilled plates.

CHAPTER 5

SEAFOOD ENTREES

Scallop Nachos

Nachos are traditionally an appetizer of deep-fried corn tortilla chips with melted cheese and chopped jalapeños; beef, pork or chicken are added to make a more substantial dish. In this rendition, the corn chips are replaced by small arrows of the finer—but still earthy—thick flour tortillas known as gorditas ("little fatties"; see page 196). Or you can use regular flour tortillas. In place of Monterey Jack or Cheddar, I use a Roquefort Cream Sauce, which complements the scallops.

TO SERVE 6

▼◲ *Roquefort Cream Sauce*

3 cups heavy cream
6 ounces Roquefort cheese, crumbled
1 teaspoon white pepper

▼◲ *Scallop Nachos*

3 gorditas or regular flour tortillas
24 large sea scallops (about 2 pounds total), tough white connective tissue trimmed off
2 tablespoons vegetable oil
½ teaspoon white pepper
¼ teaspoon kosher salt
6 ounces Green Sorrel Indian Paint (page 210)

For the Roquefort Cream Sauce: Bring the cream to a boil in a medium saucepan over moderate-to-high heat. Add the Roquefort and pepper and cook at a low rolling boil, stirring occasionally, until reduced by half, about 25 minutes. Pass the sauce through a sieve. Return it to the saucepan, set it aside and keep it warm.

For the Scallop Nachos: While the sauce is reducing, prepare the nachos. Preheat the oven to 425°F. Cut the gorditas in half. Cut each half into 4 wedges. Then trim each wedge into a triangular "arrow." Wrap the 24 arrows in a single layer in a sheet of aluminum foil and heat them in the oven for about 4 minutes, just until warmed through.

Preheat the grill or broiler. Pat the scallops dry, coat them with the oil and sprinkle with pepper and salt. Lightly oil the grill or broiler tray and cook the scallops about 3 inches from the heat for 2 minutes, then turn them and cook for 30 seconds longer—they should be lightly golden and still soft to the touch.

Spoon 4 tablespoons of the sauce into the center of each large heated serving plate. Place 4 arrows parallel along one side of the plate, pointing inward and half overlapping the sauce. On the other side of the sauce, place 4 scallops, parallel to the arrows. Put the Green Sorrel Indian Paint into a squeeze bottle and paint a jagged line across the plate between the scallops and tortilla arrows; punctuate the line with 3 dots of paint.

Scallop Nachos

Boudins of Scallops with Fennel Served with Blue Cornmeal Fettucini and a Tomato Reduction

Boudin is French for sausage, appropriate for these light, smooth seafood sausages flavored with fennel seed. I serve them with distinctively Southwestern accompaniments—fresh blue cornmeal pasta and a pastel tomato sauce.

TO SERVE 6

◄◻ Boudin of Scallops with Fennel

1 pound sea scallops, trimmed
  of tough membranes and
  patted dry
7 ounces heavy cream
1 egg
1 egg white
2 teaspoons fennel seed
1 teaspoon white pepper

For the Boudins of Scallops: Put the scallops in a processor and pulse to chop them coarsely. With the motor running, add the cream and continue processing until the scallops are smoothly pureed. Pulse in the egg, egg white, fennel seed and pepper. Scrape the scallop mousse into a metal bowl and chill it in the refrigerator for 1 hour.

Place a 2½-foot-long sheet of plastic wrap on the work surface. Spoon the scallop mousse evenly down the center of the plastic wrap in a line 1 inch wide and ending 1 inch from either end of the sheet. Fold the lower half of the plastic over the line of mousse; then roll up the plastic fairly tightly, completely enclosing the mousse.

Tie each end of the roll in a tight knot with a 4-inch piece of kitchen string. With 2 more pieces of string, tie a pair of tight knots, ¼ to ½ inch apart, in the middle of the roll (you will cut

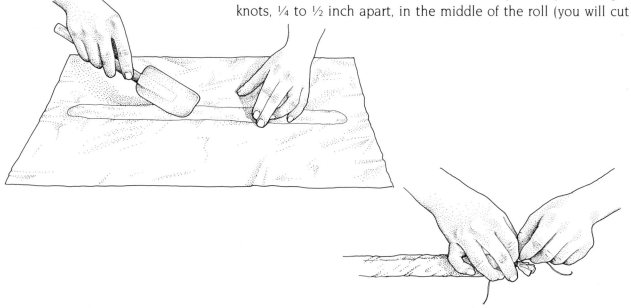

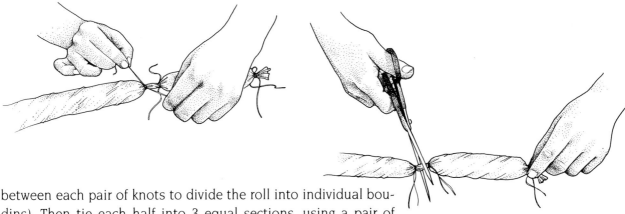

between each pair of knots to divide the roll into individual boudins). Then tie each half into 3 equal sections, using a pair of knots at each division. Cut between each pair of knots to make 6 sausages—boudins—with a knot at each end.

For the Tomato Reduction: Heat the butter in a medium saucepan over moderate heat. Add the shallot and sauté until it is transparent, about 2 minutes. Add the tomatoes, tarragon, white wine, vinegar, tomato paste, salt and pepper. Raise the heat and simmer briskly, stirring frequently, until the liquid has reduced to ½ cup, about 5 minutes. Add the cream and continue simmering until the sauce has reduced to 1½ cups, about 10 minutes. Sieve the sauce and keep it warm.

For the Blue Cornmeal Fettucini: Bring 2 quarts of water to a rolling boil with 2 tablespoons of kosher salt and 1 tablespoon of vegetable oil in a large saucepan. Add the pasta and cook it until tender but still slightly chewy (al dente), about 5 minutes. Drain the pasta well and set it aside.

Bring water to a boil in a steamer or a large pot with a steaming rack. Put the boudins in the steamer and steam until firm, about 7 minutes.

Melt the butter for the pasta in a medium saucepan over moderate heat. Add the shallot and sauté until it is transparent, about 2 minutes. Add the pasta, salt and pepper and toss the noodles well, to coat them with the butter and heat them through, about 1 minute.

Spoon the tomato reduction into the middle of each large warmed serving plate. Place a bed of pasta on top. Slip the knot from 1 end of each boudin and slip it from its casing onto the pasta.

▼ Tomato Reduction

1 tablespoon clarified butter
1 large shallot, finely chopped
3 tomatoes, peeled, seeded and coarsely chopped
5 sprigs fresh tarragon, cut into ½-inch pieces
1 cup white wine
2 tablespoons red wine vinegar
1 tablespoon tomato paste
1 teaspoon salt
½ teaspoon white pepper
2 cups heavy cream

▼ Blue Cornmeal Fettucini

1 pound Blue Cornmeal Pasta (page 203), rolled out, dried and cut into long ½-inch-wide noodles
2 tablespoons kosher salt
1 tablespoon vegetable oil
2 tablespoons unsalted butter
1 medium shallot, finely chopped
1 teaspoon salt
½ teaspoon black pepper

Tortilla Checkerboards with Mussels and Saffron

Mussels and saffron are a classic combination. In this recipe they are served with a fried checkerboard woven from strips of blue and gold tortilla, which serves the role of a crouton—a crisp accompaniment to the plump shellfish and creamy sauce.

Start with absolutely fresh raw mussels; don't use any that are already open, or have cracked shells, or that do not open when steamed. Though the recipe calls for 6 mussels per serving, I've added an extra 6 to the ingredients list to make up for any that cannot be used.

TO SERVE 6

◀▢ *Tortilla Checkerboards*
  6 blue corn tortillas
  6 gold corn tortillas
    Vegetable oil for deep frying

◀▢ *Mussels and Saffron*
  ¾ cup dry white wine
  1 large shallot, finely chopped
  1 garlic clove, finely chopped
  42 large black mussels, cleaned, bearded and scrubbed
  1½ cups heavy cream
  1 teaspoon saffron threads

For the Tortilla Checkerboards: Stack the tortillas and cut them into 3½-inch squares. Cut each square into 4 equal strips. For each checkerboard, place 4 blue strips side by side; one at a time, weave 4 gold strips between the blue strips.

Heat ¾ inch of oil in a large heavy skillet to a temperature of 425°F. on a deep-frying thermometer. Fry each checkerboard separately, holding it between a pair of metal spatulas to keep it flat as it fries; after about 1 minute, when the checkerboard is crisp enough to hold its shape, release it from the spatulas and fry for about 1 minute more, until completely cooked through and crisp. Drain the checkerboards on paper towels, pat them dry. Set aside.

For the Mussels and Saffron: Put the wine, shallot, garlic and mussels in a large, shallow saucepan over high heat. When the liquid boils, reduce the heat to moderate, cover the pan with a lid or foil, and steam the mussels until their shells open, about 5 minutes. Remove the mussels from the pan; shell them, discarding any unopened mussels, and keep them warm.

Strain the mussel cooking liquid through cheesecloth or a very fine sieve. Bring it to a boil in a medium saucepan over moderate-to-high heat; cook the liquid at a low rolling boil until it reduces to ½ cup, about 5 minutes. Add the cream and saffron and continue simmering until the sauce has reduced to 1½ cups, about 10 minutes more. Sieve the sauce again.

Spoon the sauce into the middle of each large warmed serving plate. Place a checkerboard in the center of the sauce and place 6 mussels on each plate, arranging them in 2 fans of 3 mussels each at opposite corners of the checkerboard.

Tortilla Checkerboard with Mussels and Saffron

Shrimp Enchiladas with Mustard Cream Sauce and Leeks

At Saint Estèphe we use Santa Barbara shrimp for this, or, when they're not available, Spanish red shrimp from the Mediterranean. The "staircase" shape of the tortilla cutouts was inspired by Mayan petroglyphs—stone reliefs cut on pyramids and tombs.

TO SERVE 6

◤ Mustard Cream Sauce

3 cups heavy cream
3 tablespoons extra strong Dijon mustard
½ teaspoon salt
½ teaspoon white pepper

◤ Shrimp Enchiladas

4 medium leeks, washed, tough ends trimmed
1 tablespoon unsalted butter
⅛ teaspoon salt
12 blue corn tortillas
Vegetable oil for deep frying
24 fresh medium-sized shrimp (about 1½ pounds), peeled and deveined, tails left on

For the Mustard Cream Sauce: Bring the cream to a boil in a saucepan over moderate-to-high heat and cook it over a low rolling boil until it reduces by half, about 25 minutes. Stir in the mustard, salt and pepper and keep the sauce warm.

For the Shrimp Enchiladas: While the sauce is reducing, make the enchiladas. Cut a 3-inch section from the green part of each of the leeks (reserve the white parts for another dish). Cut the leek greens lengthwise into a thin julienne. Melt the butter in a sauté pan over moderate heat and sauté the leek strips until tender-crisp, about 2 minutes. Season with salt and keep them warm.

Stacking the tortillas 2 at a time, use the tip of a small sharp knife to cut out "staircase" shapes, like two interconnecting L's, 6 inches long and about ¾ inch wide; reserve the trimmings for making tortilla chips or confetti of tortillas (page 197). Pour oil to depth of ½ inch into a large heavy skillet and heat to 375°F. on a deep-frying thermometer. Fry the cut-out tortillas for about 30 seconds, until tender, soft and flexible. Pat them dry with paper towels and set them aside.

Bring water to a boil in a steamer or a pot with a steaming rack. Place the shrimp in the steamer and cook for about 4 minutes.

Spoon the sauce into the middle of each large warmed serving plate. Place 1 tortilla cutout along one side of the sauce. Spoon the leeks on top of the tortilla and place the head ends of 4 shrimp along its length, tail ends in a fan across the plate. Place another tortilla on top of the shrimp, overlapping parallel to the first tortilla.

Shrimp Enchiladas with Mustard Cream Sauce and Leeks

Frog Legs with Gazpacho Beurre Blanc and Mousselines of Red and Green Pepper

I like the taste of frog legs. Some people compare them to chicken, which is partly true, though I think good frog legs also have a slight taste of the sea. In France, they are classically served with a garlic-and-parsley butter. I've added a distinct Southwestern variation here: a cross between a French *beurre blanc* sauce and gazpacho, the classic spicy cold soup of tomatoes, peppers, onion and garlic that is popular all over my hometown of Santa Fe.

  Buy the freshest frog legs you can find. Most of those available are imported from France or Japan, though they are now also being raised in California. (Don't use Louisiana frog legs, which I find larger and tougher.) It's funny to think that frogs are raised commercially in "herds," a word that usually makes me think of cattle roaming the plains of New Mexico.

TO SERVE 6

◤▫ Gazpacho

2 tomatoes, peeled, seeded and finely diced
4 tablespoons finely chopped cucumber
3 tablespoons finely chopped onion
3 tablespoons finely chopped green bell pepper
2 tablespoons finely chopped red bell pepper
2 tablespoons finely chopped fresh parsley
1½ teaspoons finely chopped garlic
1 teaspoon salt
1 teaspoon black pepper
3 tablespoons red wine vinegar
1 tablespoon olive oil

◤▫ Beurre Blanc

1 cup dry white wine
2 tablespoons red wine vinegar
1 teaspoon salt
½ teaspoon white pepper

For the Gazpacho: Stir together the tomatoes, cucumber, onion, peppers, parsley, garlic, salt and pepper. Stir in the vinegar and oil and leave the mixture at room temperature for 1 hour.

For the Beurre Blanc: Put the wine, vinegar, salt, pepper and shallots in a medium saucepan and bring them to a boil over moderate-to-high heat. Cook at a low rolling boil until the liquid has reduced to ¼ cup, about 15 minutes. Add the cream and boil until the liquid reduces back to ¼ cup, about 5 minutes more. With a wire whisk, briskly whisk in the butter in small pieces until it is fully incorporated. Sieve the sauce, cover it and keep it warm.

For the Mousselines of Red and Green Pepper: Put the roasted red peppers in a processor with 1 egg, 2 teaspoons of cream, and ⅛ teaspoon each of salt and pepper. Process the mixture until fine and smooth. Remove the mixture from the bowl and set it aside. Repeat the procedure with the green peppers and the remaining ingredients.

  Butter 6 small brioche molds (use ramekins or custard cups if not available). Spoon the red pepper mixture into the 6 molds, filling them halfway; then carefully spoon the green pepper mixture on top, filling them to the rim. Cover them with circles of waxed paper.

Frog Legs with Gazpacho Beurre Blanc and Mousselines of Red and Green Pepper

2 shallots, peeled, left whole
¼ cup heavy cream
12 tablespoons unsalted butter, softened

2¼ pounds fresh frog legs (about 30 pairs), feet and backbone removed, legs crossed at ankles
½ teaspoon salt
½ teaspoon white pepper
1 tablespoon all-purpose flour
¼ cup clarified butter

◣⊐ *Mousselines of Red and Green Pepper*
2 red bell peppers, roasted, peeled, stemmed and seeded (page 22)
2 green bell peppers, roasted, peeled, stemmed and seeded (page 22)
2 eggs
4 teaspoons heavy cream
¼ teaspoon salt
¼ teaspoon white pepper

Bring water to a boil in a steamer or a large pot with a steaming rack. Place the filled molds on the rack and steam them until the mousselines are set, about 6 minutes. Remove the mousselines from the steamer and let them rest while you prepare the frog legs.

For the final assembly: Preheat the oven to 400°F. Sprinkle the frog legs with salt and pepper and dust them with flour. Heat the clarified butter in a large ovenproof skillet over high heat and sauté the frog legs for 3 minutes per side, until golden. Put the skillet in the oven for 5 minutes more.

Stir the gazpacho mixture into the beurre blanc, and spoon the sauce into the middle of each large warmed serving plate. Pat the frog legs dry with paper towels and arrange them in a spoke pattern on the plates. Serve with Mousselines of Red and Green Pepper.

Tournedos of Salmon with Confetti of Tortilla

I think salmon is the meatiest fish. And, since its rich taste and texture can stand up to a wide range of accompaniments, it is my favorite to cook. In this recipe, I've done two different things with salmon that are normally reserved for beef. First with the fish itself: the recipe calls for center cuts of the fillet, which are rolled and tied into the compact shapes known in French as *tournedos*—shapes usually associated with beef fillet. And for the the sauce I use horseradish and cream, the classic accompaniments to prime ribs.

As a colorful garnish to offset the rich pink of the salmon and white of the sauce, each dish is sprinkled with a multicolored "confetti" cut from fresh flour tortillas and blue and gold corn tortillas. For the confetti, you can use scraps and trimmings, saved from other recipes in this book that use tortillas, and kept in an airtight container in the refrigerator.

TO SERVE 6

For the Confetti of Tortilla: Cut each tortilla into strips ¼ inch wide. Cut the strips diagonally into ¼-inch diamonds. Set the confetti aside.

For the Horseradish Cream Sauce: Put the wine, shallots, salt and pepper in a medium saucepan and bring them to a boil over moderate-to-high heat. Boil until the wine has reduced by half, about 10 minutes. Add the cream and grated horseradish, reduce the heat to maintain a low, rolling boil, and continue cooking the sauce until it has reduced to 1½ cups, about 20 minutes. Sieve the sauce and keep it warm.

For the Tournedos of Salmon: While the sauce is reducing, prepare the tournedos. Place each salmon fillet on its side and roll and tuck its narrow ends under to make a compact circular tournedo shape; securely tie each tournedo around its side with kitchen string.

Preheat the grill or broiler. Season each tournedo on both sides with salt and pepper, and brush with oil. Oil the grill or broiler pan and cook the tournedos about 4 inches from the heat for 4 minutes, then turn them and cook 3 minutes more until the fish is just firm in the center.

◀▫ *Confetti of Tortillas*
1 flour tortilla
1 blue corn tortilla
1 gold corn tortilla

◀▫ *Horseradish Cream Sauce*
1 cup dry white wine
2 medium shallots, finely chopped
1 teaspoon salt
1 teaspoon white pepper
2 cups heavy cream
1 2-inch piece fresh horseradish, grated

◀▫ *Tournedos of Salmon*
12 1-inch thick center cut fillets of salmon (about 3 ounces each)
1 teaspoon salt
1 teaspoon white pepper
2 tablespoons vegetable oil

Spoon the sauce into the center of each large heated serving plate. Snip the strings from the tournedos and place 2 on each plate. Sprinkle the confetti over the sauce.

Salmon Painted Desert

The pattern made by the shallot sauce and two kinds of Indian Paint reminds me of the complex striated colors of the mesas in the New Mexican desert. But the design is really very easy to make.

TO SERVE 6

◣ *Shallot Sauce*
½ cup dry white wine
1 teaspoon finely chopped shallots
2 cups heavy cream
½ teaspoon salt
½ teaspoon white pepper

◣ *Salmon*
6 6-ounce salmon steaks
½ teaspoon kosher salt
½ teaspoon white pepper
¼ cup Green Sorrel Indian Paint (page 210)
¼ cup Red Chile Indian Paint (page 209)

For the Shallot Sauce: Bring the wine and shallots to a boil in a saucepan over moderate-to-high heat and cook until the wine reduces by half, about 5 minutes. Add the cream and seasonings and continue cooking over a low rolling boil, stirring frequently with a wire whisk, until the sauce has reduced to 1½ cups, in about 15 minutes. Pass the sauce through a sieve. Set it aside and keep it warm.

For the Salmon: While the sauce is reducing, season the salmon steaks with salt and pepper. Bring water to a boil in a steamer or a large pot with a steamer rack. Steam the salmon for 5 to 7 minutes, until firm to the touch.

Just before the salmon is done, spoon the sauce into the middle of each large warmed serving plate, tilting the plate to coat it evenly to the rim. Put the Green Sorrel Indian Paint in a plastic squeeze bottle and, starting at one side of each plate, draw 8 lines about 1 inch apart, stopping about two-thirds of the way across the plate. Put the Red Chile Indian Paint in another squeeze bottle and draw 8 red lines alternating with the green lines. With the top of a knife, draw perpendicular lines about ½ inch apart through the red and green paint lines.

Place a salmon steak in the unpainted third of each plate. Serve immediately, with the salmon nearest the diner.

Top: *Salmon Painted Desert.* Top, right: *Weavings of Salmon Navajo-Style with a Green Chile Butter Sauce.* Bottom: *Tournedos of Salmon with Confetti of Tortilla*

Weavings of Salmon Navajo-Style with a Green Chile Butter Sauce

The Navajos use artistically woven baskets as food utensils. This dish was inspired by their basketry.

TO SERVE 6

12 2½-ounce salmon fillets

◤◲ *Green Chile Butter Sauce*
¼ cup red wine vinegar
2 medium shallots, finely chopped
½ teaspoon salt
½ cup dry white wine
2 cups heavy cream
4 fresh green Anaheim chiles, roasted, peeled, seeded (page 22) and finely chopped
½ cup unsalted butter

For the Weavings of Salmon: Cut each salmon fillet into strips ½ inch wide and 5 inches long. Place the strips from 1 fillet side by side to form a rectangle. One at a time, weave the strips from another fillet through the strips of the first. Set each weaving aside as you make it.

For the Green Chile Butter Sauce: Boil the vinegar, shallots and salt together in a heavy saucepan over moderate-to-high heat until reduced by half, about 3 minutes. Add the wine and reduce the liquid by half again, about 5 minutes more. Add the cream and continue cooking at a low, rolling boil until the sauce has reduced by half once more, about 15 minutes. Whisk in the chiles and butter, and press the sauce through a sieve. Set the sauce aside and keep it warm.

Bring water to a boil in a steamer or a pot with a steaming rack. Place the weavings of salmon in the steamer, making certain they do not touch the water. Steam them for 3 minutes, just until firm. Remove to a plate covered with paper towels and pat off excess moisture.

Spoon the sauce into the middle of each large heated serving plate and place a weaving of salmon in the center of the plate on top of the sauce.

Jou de Lotte "Fish and Chips" with Sorrel Sauce

Lotte, also known as monkfish and anglerfish, has recently become popular, largely because its firm texture and rich flavor are reminiscent of lobster. Jou de lotte are the fish's cheeks, tender delicate little chunks of flesh that I like to serve with fish-shaped vegetables and crisp tortilla chips in a playful Southwestern version of fish and chips. Ask your fishmonger to save you the lotte cheeks, or, if not available, replace them in the recipe with 3 2-inch pieces of lotte per serving.

TO SERVE 6

For the Sorrel Sauce: Melt the butter in a medium saucepan over moderate heat. Add the shallots and sauté them just until tender, about 2 minutes. Add the sorrel and sauté until the leaves melt, 2 to 3 minutes more. Transfer the sorrel mixture to a processor and add the salt, pepper, fish stock and cream; process until the mixture is smoothly pureed. Then sieve the sauce and set it aside.

For the "Fish and Chips": Cut ⅓-inch-thick strips from the sides of the summer squash, zucchini and carrot. With the tip of a small, sharp knife, carve the strips to make 3 1½-inch-long fish from each vegetable. Bring 1 quart of water to a boil with 1 tablespoon of salt in a medium saucepan over moderate-to-high heat. Add the carrot "fish" and cook them until tender-crisp, about 3 minutes; remove them with a slotted spoon and drain them on paper towels. Add the yellow squash and zucchini to the saucepan and cook them for 2 minutes, then drain.

With the tip of a small, sharp knife, cut 3 2-inch-long fish shapes from each tortilla. Heat 2 inches of oil in a deep fryer or a large heavy skillet to a temperature of 425°F. on a deep-frying thermometer. Add the cut-out tortillas and fry them until crisp but not browned, about 45 seconds. Drain the tortilla chips well on paper towels.

For the Jou de Lotte: Preheat a grill or broiler until very hot. Season the jou de lotte or lotte pieces with salt and pepper and brush them with olive oil. Grill or broil them about 3 inches from the heat for about 1½ minutes per side.

While the fish is grilling, heat the sauce through in a medium saucepan over moderate-to-high heat. Spoon the sauce down

◥◣ Sorrel Sauce
1 tablespoon unsalted butter
2 medium shallots, coarsely chopped
6 bunches sorrel, stemmed and coarsely chopped
½ teaspoon salt
½ teaspoon white pepper
1 cup Fish Stock (page 211)
½ cup heavy cream

◥◣ "Fish and Chips"
2 yellow summer squash
1 large zucchini
1 large carrot, peeled
6 blue corn tortillas
6 gold corn tortillas
Vegetable oil for deep frying

◥◣ Jou de Lotte (or other parts of lotte)
18 jou de lotte, about 2 ounces each
½ teaspoon salt
½ teaspoon white pepper
2 tablespoons olive oil

lou de Lotte "Fish and Chips" with Sorrel Sauce

along one side of each large heated serving plate. Place 3 jou de lotte per plate on top of the sauce. Place the fish-shaped vegetables on top of the jou de lotte. Arrange the blue and gold tortilla-chip fish on the other side of the plate.

Pecos River Trout with Verdolagas, Lardons and Pine Nuts

When I was very young, my dad took me trout fishing in the icy waters of the Pecos River, high in the Sangre de Cristo Mountains. The crisp air, the deer and the small rabbits we saw, the scent of the aspen trees—all created an unforgettable picture in my memory. And fresh brook trout cooked over an open fire became one of my ideals of perfect, simple cooking.

Bacon is a classic accompaniment to pan-fried trout, and the earthy flavor of blue cornmeal makes an excellent coating for the fish's delicate flesh. I like to add the succulent greens of verdolagas, which grow abundantly in the Southwest after the spring and summer rains. If verdolagas are beyond your reach, substitute watercress. It won't be the same, but it is another lovely combination.

TO SERVE 6

Rinse the trout under cold running water; don't dry them. Salt and pepper their insides. Spread the cornmeal on a large flat plate and dredge the trout in the cornmeal to coat them.

Heat the oil in a large heavy skillet over moderate-to-high heat. Add the bacon and sauté it until almost all its fat has been rendered and the pieces are lightly browned but not yet crisp, about 3 minutes. Leaving all the fat in the skillet, drain the bacon on paper towels.

Place the trout in the skillet in a single layer, without crowding them (cook them in 2 batches if necessary). Fry them on one side over moderate-to-high heat until golden, about 4 minutes; turn them over, reduce the heat to moderate, and cook them about 5 minutes more. Carefully remove the trout from the skillet and drain them on paper towels.

Pour all but a very thin coating of fat from the skillet. Return

6 whole brook trout, about
  10 ounces each, cleaned
½ teaspoon salt
½ teaspoon white pepper
1 cup blue cornmeal
¼ cup vegetable oil
¼ pound thickly sliced cured
  bacon, cut into 1-inch pieces
2 medium shallots, finely
  chopped
¼ cup pine nuts, toasted
  (page 24)
2 bunches verdolagas, rinsed,
  leaves left in small clusters
  (see above)

Pecos River Trout with Verdolagas, Lardons and Pine Nuts

the bacon to the skillet with the shallots and sauté over moderate heat just until the shallots are soft, about 1 minute; add the pine nuts and sauté about 30 seconds more to warm them through. Then toss in the verdolagas, give a quick stir to warm them, and arrange them, with the bacon and pine nuts, over the trout on large, warmed serving plates.

Southwest Bouillabaisse with Nopalitos and Red Chile

The traditional bouillabaisse of Mediterranean France is a generous main-course fisherman's soup. It features a sampling of the day's catch—fish and shellfish simmered together in a white wine broth fragrant with saffron. In this Southwestern version, there is just as wide a selection of fresh fish as you'll find in the south of France. The broth, however, has the distinctive local flavors of red chile and green nopal cactus to enhance its fragrance. Whole roasted chile pods and an edible "lobster claw" of grilled nopal add a final touch of the desert to this seafood specialty.

Use the fish listed below as your guide to buying appropriate quantities of whatever varieties are best at your local fish market. Plan on a total of 15 ounces of seafood for each generous portion. Be sure to ask your fishmonger, in advance if necessary, to save you the cod or halibut bones necessary to give good flavor to the broth.

TO SERVE 6

For the Southwest Bouillabaisse: Heat the olive oil in a large deep stockpot over moderate heat. Add the garlic and sauté it, stirring frequently, until soft but not browned, about 3 minutes. Add the carrots, celery, onions, orange peel, bay leaves, parsley, thyme, salt, anise seed and peppercorns; sauté, stirring frequently, until the onions are translucent, 7 to 10 minutes. Add the chiles and sauté for about 1 minute more.

Add the fish bones, tomatoes, cactus strips, lemon, water, wine and tomato paste. Stir well, raise the heat to high and bring the liquid to a boil. Reduce the heat and simmer briskly until the liquid has reduced by half, about 1½ hours. Pour the soup through a fine sieve to remove all the solids from the broth.

¼ cup olive oil
6 medium garlic cloves, finely chopped
3 medium carrots, peeled and cut into 1-inch pieces
3 medium celery stalks, cut into 1-inch pieces
2 medium onions, cut into ½-inch chunks
Peel of 1 orange, rind part only
3 bay leaves
1 bunch parsley, coarsely chopped

1 teaspoon fresh thyme (or
  2 teaspoons dried)
1 teaspoon salt
½ teaspoon whole anise seed
½ teaspoon whole black
  peppercorns
4 mild dried red chile pods (4 to
  5 inches each)
2 pounds cod or halibut bones
4 medium tomatoes, cut into
  1-inch pieces
3 medium nopal cactus pads,
  scraped, trimmed, cut
  crosswise into 1-inch strips,
  parboiled and rinsed
  thoroughly (page 24)
½ lemon, cut into 2 pieces
1 gallon water
3 cups dry white wine
5 tablespoons tomato paste
12 medium sea scallops, tough
  white membranes trimmed off
  (about 9 ounces total)
2 6-ounce fillets of cod, seabass,
  redfish, or other firm-fleshed
  white fish, cut into 3 pieces
  each
6 medium-sized fresh shrimp
  (about 6 ounces total), peeled
  and deveined, tails left on
6 ounces fresh chunk crabmeat
1 dozen small fresh clams in
  their shells, cleaned
1 dozen medium-sized black
  mussels, in their shells, cleaned

◤ Cactus Claw Garnish

6 medium nopal cactus pads,
  scraped and trimmed (page
  24) and cut into 3-pronged
  claw shapes
1 tablespoon olive oil
1 large garlic clove, finely
  chopped
1 teaspoon black pepper
½ teaspoon salt
6 mild dried red chile pods (4 to
  5 inches each)

Return the broth to the stockpot and bring it back to a gentle simmer. Add the scallops, fish fillets, shrimp and crabmeat and cook to medium—just until the fish flakes—for about 4 minutes. Remove the seafood with a slotted spoon and distribute evenly among 6 large shallow heated soup plates. Add the clams and mussels to the broth and cook just until their shells open, about 3 minutes. Remove with a slotted spoon and distribute them evenly among the plates. Keep the fish and shellfish warm; keep the broth at the simmer.

For the Cactus Claw Garnish: While the seafood is cooking, preheat the grill or broiler. Combine the olive oil and garlic and brush them all over the claw-shaped nopal pads. Season the pads with the pepper and salt. Grill or broil the cactus claws as close as possible to the heat, about 2 inches away, for about 1 minute per side, until tender but still bright green in color. During the last 20 seconds or so, add the chiles.

Ladle the hot broth over each serving of seafood and garnish each serving with a cactus claw and a chile pod, both extending over the rim of the soup plate.

Southwest Bouillabaisse with Nopalitos and Red Chile

CHAPTER 6

POULTRY ENTREES

Roast Pheasant with a Stuffing of Blue Cornbread, Candied Lime and Chiles, Served with a Lime Cream Sauce

Combining earthy, spicy and sweet flavors, this stuffing is wonderful for all kinds of poultry. Try it with turkey for a Southwestern-style Thanksgiving.

TO SERVE 6

For the Stuffing: Put the lime juice, lime zest and sugar in a small saucepan over moderate-to-high heat. Bring them to a boil, reduce the heat and simmer until the zest is coated with a thick syrup, about 10 minutes. Set the candied lime zest aside.

Melt the butter in a medium skillet over moderate heat. Add the jalapeños and sauté them just until tender-crisp, about 4 minutes.

In a mixing bowl, combine the candied lime, jalapeños, blue corn bread cubes, raisins and chicken stock.

Season the cavities of the pheasants with salt and pepper. Fill them with the stuffing. Make 6 triple-folded strips of aluminum foil about 8 inches long and ½ inch wide. Use a strip of foil to bind together the drumstick ends of each pheasant's legs. Twist the wing joints of each pheasant, tucking them under so they stay in place during roasting.

Preheat the oven to 375°F.

For the Lime Cream Sauce: Put the chicken stock and lime juice in a medium saucepan and bring them to a boil over moderate-to-high heat. Reduce the heat and cook the liquid over a low, rolling boil until it reduces to 1½ cups, about 30 minutes. Add the cream and continue boiling until the sauce has reduced back to 1½ cups, about 20 minutes more. Stir in the chile pequín.

While the sauce is reducing, roast the pheasants until their skin is golden brown and their juices run slightly pink when the thigh is pierced with a thin skewer, 15 to 20 minutes. Spoon the sauce into the middle of each large warmed serving plate. Remove the foil strip from each pheasant and place the bird on top of the sauce.

☞ The Stuffing
½ cup lime juice
¼ cup lime zest
¼ cup sugar
1 tablespoon unsalted butter
6 fresh red jalapeños (or green, if red are unavailable), stemmed, seeded and cut into ⅛-inch dice (about ½ cup total)
1 recipe Blue Cornbread (page 197), cooled and cut into ½-inch cubes
⅓ cup seedless raisins
¼ cup Chicken Stock (page 211)

6 small pheasants (about 1 pound each)
½ teaspoon salt
½ teaspoon black pepper

☞ Lime Cream Sauce
3 cups Chicken Stock (page 211)
1 cup fresh lime juice
1 cup heavy cream
1 teaspoon chile pequín (available in Latin markets)

Breast of Chicken with Passionfruit Butter and Blue Cornbread Cobs

The desert and the tropics meet in this dish, the dense cobs of blue cornbread in contrast to the tart-sweet, sprightly flavor of the passionfruit. To me, passionfruit seeds look like black caviar, and as a garnish they give this recipe's presentation an extra touch of elegance.

TO SERVE 6

For the Passionfruit Butter: Put the wine, vinegar and shallot in a medium saucepan and bring them to a boil over moderate-to-high heat. Cook them at a low rolling boil until reduced by half, about 10 minutes. Add the cream and continue boiling until the sauce reduces back to ½ cup, about 10 minutes more. Set the sauce aside.

For the Chicken Breasts:

Preheat the oven to 375°F.

While the sauce is reducing, season the chicken breasts all over with the salt and pepper and brush them with the oil. Put them on a baking sheet and bake them for about 17 minutes, until lightly golden.

When the sauce has reduced, whisk in the butter in pieces, then whisk in the seeds of the 9 passionfruit. Sieve the sauce and keep it warm.

Slice each chicken breast at a 45-degree angle into ¼-inch-thick pieces. Fan the pieces of 1 breast across the lower half of each large warmed serving plate. Place a blue cornbread cob across the top half. Spoon the sauce over the breast slices, and garnish each breast with a sprinkling of the additional passionfruit seeds and pulp.

☞ *Passionfruit Butter*

1 cup dry white wine
1 teaspoon red wine vinegar
1 medium shallot, finely chopped
½ cup heavy cream
¾ pound unsalted butter
9 passionfruit, halved, seeds and pulp scooped out and reserved

☞ *Breast of Chicken*

6 8-ounce boneless chicken breasts, first joint of the wing bones attached
1 teaspoon salt
1 teaspoon white pepper
2 tablespoons vegetable oil
¼ recipe Blue Cornbread, baked in corncob molds (page 197)
2 passionfruit, halved, seeds and pulp scooped out and reserved, for garnish

Breast of Chicken with Passionfruit Butter and Blue Cornbread Cob

Breast of Chicken with Jícama and Jalapeño Vinegar Sauce

Jícama, a homely root whose lumpy light-brown skin conceals crisp, juicy, slightly sweet white flesh, is popular throughout the Southwest. You often see people eating it as a snack, peeled, cut into sticks and seasoned with a squeeze of fresh lime and a dusting of salt and chile powder. Here, matchsticks of jícama combine with a sharp and spicy sauce with homemade jalapeño vinegar to enhance a light, sprightly chicken dish that is a favorite at Saint Estèphe. If possible, have your butcher prepare boned chicken breasts for you with the first joint of the wing bone still attached, for a more attractive presentation.

TO SERVE 6

Jalapeño Vinegar Sauce
6 tablespoons Jalapeño Vinegar (page 203)
3 cups heavy cream
½ cup Duck Stock (page 212) or Chicken Stock (page 211)

Breasts of Chicken and Jícama
6 8-ounce boneless chicken breasts, first joint of the wing bones attached
2 teaspoons salt
2 teaspoons white pepper
1 tablespoon vegetable oil
1 medium jícama, peeled
1½ tablespoons unsalted butter
2 large carrots for Carrot Tulip garnish (optional)

For the Jalapeño Vinegar Sauce: Boil the vinegar in a small saucepan over moderate-to-high heat until it has reduced by half, about 5 minutes. Add the cream and stock, bring them to a boil, then lower the heat and cook at a low, rolling boil, stirring occasionally, until the sauce has reduced to 1½ cups, about 25 minutes. Keep the sauce warm.

For the Breasts of Chicken and Jícama: Preheat the oven to 400°F. While the sauce reduces, prepare the chicken and jícama. Season the chicken breasts with 1 teaspoon each of the salt and pepper and brush them with the oil. Place them, skin side up, on an oiled baking sheet and plump up each one with your fingers to give it a nice, rounded shape. Bake for about 12 minutes, until lightly browned, then remove the breasts from the oven and cover with foil to keep them warm.

Cut the jícama into ¼-inch-thick slices. Stack the slices a few at a time and cut them into ¼-inch-wide sticks. Melt the butter in a skillet over moderate heat, add the jícama and the remaining salt and pepper and sauté for 2 to 3 minutes, just until heated through. Spoon the jícama in a mound on one side of each large heated serving plate. Place a chicken breast on top and spoon the sauce over the breast. If desired, cut 3 cup-shaped "tulips" from each carrot. Decorate the other side of each plate with a carrot tulip.

Breast of Chicken with Jícama and Jalapeño Vinegar Sauce

☞ *Grilled Boneless Squab*

6 squabs, about 10 ounces
    each, split and boned
1 teaspoon salt
1 teaspoon black pepper
2 tablespoons vegetable oil

them in a bowl with the heavy cream. Leave them to soak for about 1½ hours, until they have given their color to the cream. Lightly whip the cream to soft peaks and put it in a plastic squeeze bottle.

For the Grilled Boneless Squab: Preheat the grill or broiler until medium-hot. Lightly sprinkle both sides of the squabs with the salt and pepper and brush them with the vegetable oil. Brush the grill or broiler pan with oil and cook the squabs skin side up, about 3 inches from the heat, for about 6 minutes; turn them and cook for about 5 minutes more (the breasts should be medium rare, their juices still slightly pink if pierced with a thin skewer). Spoon the sauce slightly to one side of each large heated serving plate. Place a squab on one side of the sauce with its drumsticks near the rim of the plate. With the squeeze bottle, paint a jagged arrow across the other side of the plate and slightly overlapping the sauce, with an arrowhead at one end and a few angled parallel lines at the other to suggest feathers.

Duck with Posole
and a Sauce of Taos Valley Red Wine and Garlic

I learned to prepare duck this way from the late Jean Bertranou at L'Ermitage restaurant in Los Angeles.

Ask your butcher to separate the breasts and legs for you from a large-breasted variety of duck such as Mulard or Muscovy; each breast half should weigh at least 6 ounces. Don't use Long Island ducks; their breasts are too scrawny. Even better, buy 3 whole ducks and have the butcher separate the breasts and legs for you. Use the entire carcass to make duck stock for the sauce before you prepare the dish.

Bertranou's sauce was made with Médoc; for this recipe, I use one of the full-bodied red wines now being produced in New Mexico's Taos Valley. You can use any good, full-bodied dry red wine.

TO SERVE 6

For the Duck with Posole: Preheat the oven to 500°F. Season the duck breast halves and legs with salt and pepper. Heat the oil in a large heavy ovenproof skillet over high heat. Add the duck pieces skin side up and sear them for about 2 minutes. Then put the skillet in the oven and cook the duck for about 10 minutes more. Remove the breasts, which should be done rare, and keep them warm. Cook the legs an additional 10 minutes, until they are medium-rare; remove them from the oven and keep them warm.

For the Taos Valley Red Wine and Garlic Sauce: Pour off all but a thin coat of fat from the skillet in which the duck was cooked. Sauté the garlic in the skillet over moderate heat for about 1 minute, stirring constantly; do not let the garlic burn. Add the wine and stock; stir and scrape the skillet to dissolve the bits in the bottom of the pan, and bring the liquid to a boil. Adjust the heat to maintain a low, rolling boil and cook the sauce until it has reduced to 1½ cups, about 35 minutes. Pass the sauce through a sieve and keep it warm.

Put the posole in a small saucepan and warm it over moderate heat, about 3 to 5 minutes.

Pull the skin from the duck breasts and reserve for Duck Chicharrones Salad (page 109). Place each breast flat on a carving board and, with a very sharp knife, slice it almost parallel to the board into 4 or 5 thin slices. Place each sliced breast in a fan across the middle of a large warmed serving plate. Pat the duck legs dry with paper towels and place one above each breast fan. Spoon the sauce over the sliced breasts, and sprinkle the posole on top.

Duck with Posole

6 boneless duck breast halves and legs (with bones), from 3 large-breasted ducks
1 teaspoon salt
1 teaspoon black pepper
¼ cup vegetable oil
½ cup cooked posole (page 196)

Taos Valley Red Wine and Garlic Sauce

6 large garlic cloves, finely chopped
3 cups Taos Valley cabernet, or other full-bodied dry red wine
2 cups Duck Stock (page 212) or Veal Stock (page 212)

Tacos of Duck, Artichoke and Papaya with Green Peppercorn Vinaigrette

This is as close as I come to the conventional taco in Modern Southwest Cuisine. It includes a crisp taco shell made from a blue corn tortilla; cooked meat, in this case rare duck leg; and salad vegetables, here radicchio, Belgian endive and artichoke hearts. In addition, I've included the fresh, sweet taste of papaya for contrast. And in place of a salsa, I dress these tacos with a vinaigrette seasoned with pickled green peppercorns, a classic flavoring for duck.

TO SERVE 6

⩫ Green Peppercorn Vinaigrette

2 tablespoons pickled green peppercorns, with 1 tablespoon of their brine
1 tablespoon sherry vinegar
½ teaspoon salt
½ teaspoon black pepper
4 tablespoons hazelnut oil

⩫ Tacos of Duck, Artichoke and Papaya

3 medium artichokes
1 tablespoon kosher salt
1 papaya
1 tablespoon vegetable oil
6 duck legs (preferably Mulard or Muscovy ducks)
½ teaspoon salt
½ teaspoon black pepper
12 thin blue corn tortillas
Vegetable oil for deep frying
4 heads Belgian endive, cored and torn into bite-size pieces
2 heads radicchio, torn into bite-size pieces

For the Green Peppercorn Vinaigrette: Stir together the peppercorns and brine, vinegar, salt and pepper, until the salt dissolves. Then briskly stir in the oil. Set the dressing aside.

For the Tacos of Duck, Artichoke and Papaya: Starting at the bottom of each artichoke, snap off its leaves until only the narrow central cone of light-colored leaves remains. With a small, sharp knife, pare off the tough dark green skin of the artichoke bottoms.

Bring 1 quart of water to a boil with 1 tablespoon of kosher salt in a medium saucepan over moderate-to-high heat. Add the pared artichokes and cook them until they are tender enough for their bases to be pierced easily with the tip of a small sharp knife, about 15 minutes.

Drain the artichokes and let them cool. Then cut off the tops of the leaves, leaving about 1½ inch at the base and, with a small spoon, scoop out the fibrous chokes. Pull off the remaining leaves and pare the artichoke bottoms. Cut each artichoke bottom into 3 horizontal slices, then cut the slices into ¼-inch-thick matchsticks. Set them aside.

Halve the papaya, scoop out its seeds and fibrous strings, peel it, and cut it lengthwise into ¼-inch slices. Cut each slice crosswise into ¼-inch matchsticks and set them aside.

Preheat the oven to 400°F. Heat the tablespoon of vegetable oil in a medium-size ovenproof skillet over moderate-to-high heat. Season the duck legs with salt and pepper and put them in

Tacos of Duck, Artichoke and Papaya with Green Peppercorn Vinaigrette

the skillet; sauté them for 2 minutes, turn them over, and put the skillet into the oven. Roast the duck legs until medium rare, about 10 minutes. Drain them on paper towels. When they are cool enough to handle, remove the skin and cut the meat into bite-size pieces.

Place the tortillas in a wire taco form, or fold them and secure their edges with a toothpick. Heat enough oil to cover the tortillas in a deep, large heavy skillet or deep fryer to a temperature of 425°F. on a deep-frying thermometer. Fry the tortillas until crisp but not browned, about 45 seconds. Drain them on paper towels.

Put the dressing in a medium skillet over moderate heat. Add the duck, artichoke and papaya and toss them in the dressing just until warmed through, about 1 minute. Pour the contents of the skillet into a mixing bowl and toss them with the endive and radicchio. Fill the taco shells with the mixture and serve the tacos at once.

CHAPTER 7

MEAT ENTREES

Veal Steaks with Yucca Root and Grapefruit Sauce

The presentation of this dish is like an abstract New Mexican landscape, with blue corn tortillas and yucca root cut to resemble mountain peaks and an oblong of blue cornbread like a low adobe dwelling. The grapefruit sauce offers a zesty counterpoint to the delicate flavor of the veal and the earthiness of the yucca (a dense, potato-like tuber), tortillas and cornbread.

TO SERVE 6

For the Grapefruit Sauce: Remove the zest from 2 of the grapefruits with a zester or vegetable peeler, and reserve. Juice all 3 grapefruits. Bring the grapefruit juice to a boil in a medium saucepan over moderate heat and simmer briskly until it reduces to ⅓ cup, about 10 minutes. Stir in the stock, honey and chile, raise the heat and bring the sauce just to the boil, then remove it from the heat and keep it warm.

For the Yucca Root, Tortillas and Cornbread: Cut 10 slices about ⅓ inch thick from the yucca root (you'll only need 6, but some may break during cooking). Trim them into triangles about 2 inches tall. Bring 1 quart of water to a boil with 1 teaspoon of kosher salt in a medium saucepan. Reduce the heat to moderate-to-high. Add the yucca triangles and cook them for about 10 minutes, until tender. Drain the yucca triangles and transfer them to a bowl of ice water to stop the cooking. Pat them dry and set aside.

Cut each tortilla in half. Trim the halves with the tip of a small sharp knife to a profile of 3 connected triangular mountain peaks of different heights; reserve the trimmings for tortilla chips or confetti of tortillas (pages 197 and 127).

Preheat the oven to 400°F. Wrap the rectangles of cornbread separately in aluminum foil and heat them in the oven for about 10 minutes.

While the cornbread is heating, heat ½ inch of oil in a deep fryer or large heavy skillet to a temperature of 375°F. on a deep-frying thermometer. Fry the tortilla mountains for about 30 seconds, until tender, soft and flexible. Remove them with a slotted spoon or wire skimmer and pat them dry with paper towels. Next,

▼▫ *Grapefruit Sauce*
3 large grapefruits (preferably pink)
1 cup Veal Stock (page 212)
4 tablespoons honey
1 teaspoon chile pequín (available in Latin markets)

▼▫ *Yucca Root, Tortillas and Blue Cornbread* •
1 medium yucca root, peeled
1 teaspoon kosher salt
3 7-inch blue corn tortillas
½ loaf Blue Cornbread (page 197), trimmed and cut into 6 rectangles ¾-by-1-by-3 inches each
Vegetable oil for deep frying
¼ teaspoon salt

▼▫ *Veal Steaks*
12 2-ounce veal loin steaks (about ¾ inch thick)
1 teaspoon salt
1 teaspoon white pepper
½ cup all-purpose flour
3 tablespoons clarified butter

Veal Steaks with Yucca Root and Grapefruit Sauce

fry the yucca triangles for about 1½ minutes, until golden. Remove them and pat them dry with paper towels. Sprinkle them with the salt.

For the Veal Steaks: Season the steaks with salt and pepper and dredge them with the flour. Heat the clarified butter in a skillet over high heat. Add the veal steaks and sear them for about 1 minute; then turn them over and cook about 3 minutes more, until they are a light golden brown and cooked medium (if you slice a corner of a steak, it should be slightly pink inside).

Place a tortilla mountainscape along the top third of each large heated serving plate, with a triangle of yucca alongside. About 1 inch below the tortilla and just to the left of center, place a rectangle of blue cornbread. Spoon some sauce in a pool in the lower right of the plate and place 2 veal steaks on top.

Veal Chops Marinated in Burnt Chile Pesto with Sopaipillas and Rio Grande Honey

Have your butcher prepare the chops for you from a 6-bone rack of veal, trimming off all the fat from the rack. Any meat trimming can be reserved for making stock.

Each finished grilled chop is garnished with a whole grilled red chile—the same sort that goes into the marinade. Placed on the plate straight from the grill, the chile gives off a wonderfully intense aroma that reaches the guest before the plate does.

At Saint Estèphe, we serve the sopaipillas with mesquite honey from the Rio Grande. You can use any good-quality dark honey.

TO SERVE 6

◥◪ *Burnt Chile Pesto Marinade*
8 large dried red chiles, wiped clean with a dry cloth, stemmed, veined and seeded (page 22)
3 medium garlic cloves
¼ cup water

For the Burnt Chile Pesto Marinade: Preheat the oven to 400°F. Put the chiles in a baking tray and roast them until brittle and slightly blackened, about 1 minute. Put the chiles and garlic in a processor and process until the chiles resemble a coarse powder and the garlic is finely chopped. With the motor running, pour in the water, oil and salt.

For the Veal Chops: Rub the veal chops with the marinade. Cover the chops and leave them in the refrigerator overnight.

Before cooking the veal chops, prepare the Sopaipillas and keep them warm.

Preheat the grill or broiler. Scrape the marinade from the chops and rub them with the vegetable oil. Lightly oil the grill or broiler tray and cook the chops about 3 inches from the heat until medium-rare, about 7 minutes per side. About 30 seconds before the chops are done, heat the chiles on the grill.

Meanwhile, bring the veal stock and oregano to a boil in a saucepan over moderate-to-high heat.

Spoon the reduced stock into the middle of each large warmed serving plate. Place a veal chop on one side of the plate, overlapping the stock, with the rib bone pointing toward the rim. Place a chile and 2 sopaipillas at the top of the plate, just touching the edge of the sauce (the thickened stock). Accompany each serving with a small ramekin holding 4 tablespoons of honey and let each guest puncture the sopaipillas and spoon the honey inside them. Serve the extra sopaipillas in a napkin-lined basket.

¼ cup vegetable oil
1 teaspoon salt

Veal Chops

1 6-bone veal rack (about 3½ pounds), trimmed and cut into 6 chops
1 recipe Sopaipillas (page 198)
3 tablespoons vegetable oil
3 cups Veal Stock (page 212), boiled and reduced to 1½ cups
1 teaspoon oregano
6 large dried red chiles, wiped clean with a dry cloth and left whole
1½ cups honey

Chile con Queso with Sweetbreads

Chile con queso in its most basic Southwestern form is a dip of melted cheese, usually Monterey Jack or a processed Cheddar, spiced with chiles and served with corn chips. In this recipe, I've transformed the concept into a more delicate sauce to accompany veal sweetbreads. I like to use a good quality Parmesan-type cheese as the *queso*, and at Saint Estèphe we've been getting excellent results with an Argentine variety, Reggianito. To give the dish some spice without overpowering the other ingredients, I avoid the green jalapeños usually associated with chile con queso, and use somewhat milder fresh red jalapeños or green Anaheim chiles instead.

TO SERVE 6

1½ pounds veal sweetbreads

Chile con Queso

5 ounces finely grated Parmesan or other mild grating cheese
3 cups heavy cream
2 medium garlic cloves, coarsely chopped
1 teaspoon white pepper
1 teaspoon salt
6 small fresh red jalapeño peppers, or 3 fresh green Anaheim chiles, roasted, peeled, seeded (page 22) and left whole
½ teaspoon black pepper

For the Sweetbreads: Bring 2 quarts of water with ½ tablespoon of salt to a boil in a large saucepan. Reduce the heat, carefully slip in the sweetbreads and cook them for 30 minutes.

When the sweetbreads are almost done, prepare a bowl of ice water. Drain the sweetbreads and plunge them quickly into the ice water to stop the cooking. Carefully pull off any clear membrane from the sweetbreads and cut them into 1½-inch pieces. Set them aside.

For the Chile con Queso: While the sweetbreads are cooking, put the cheese, cream, garlic, pepper and ½ teaspoon of salt in a medium saucepan and bring to a boil over moderate-to-high heat. Boil briskly until the sauce has reduced to 1½ cups, 15 to 20 minutes. Sieve the sauce and keep it warm.

Season the sweetbreads and the peppers with the remaining ½ teaspoon of salt, and sprinkle the sweetbreads with the black pepper. Bring water to a boil in a steamer or a large pot with a steaming rack. Steam the sweetbreads and peppers until warmed through, about 4 minutes.

Spoon the sauce into the middle of each large warmed serving plate. Pat the sweetbread pieces dry with paper towels and place a cluster of them in the center of each plate. Drape the peppers over the sweetbreads.

Chile con Queso with Sweetbreads

Enchilada of Filet Mignon with Chanterelles and Sorrel Sauce

Enchilada of Filet Mignon with Chanterelles and Sorrel Sauce

While researching the cooking of the Mayas, I learned that they often painted bright designs on their tortillas with vegetable or fruit dyes. I decided to try branding tortillas with a hot skewer to make abstract patterns, and found the result an ideal way to decorate an enchilada of filet mignon.

TO SERVE 6

For the Sorrel Sauce: Melt the butter in a medium saucepan over moderate heat. Add the shallots and sauté them just until tender, about 2 minutes. Add the sorrel and sauté it until the leaves melt, 2 to 3 minutes more. Transfer the sorrel mix to a processor and add the salt, pepper and veal stock; process the mixture until it is smoothly pureed. Sieve the sauce and set it aside.

For the Enchilada of Filet Mignon with Chanterelles: Heat the tip of a metal skewer on an open flame or under a broiler until red hot. Holding the skewer with a towel, use its tip to slowly burn a decorative pattern of lines, zigzags and arrows on 6 of the tortillas, reheating the skewer as necessary. Set the tortillas aside.

Preheat the grill or broiler until very hot. Season the filets with half of the salt and pepper and brush them with the oil. Grill or broil them about 3 inches from the heat until medium-rare, 3 to 4 minutes per side.

Meanwhile, heat the sorrel sauce in a medium saucepan over moderate-to-high heat.

Melt the butter in a medium skillet over moderate-to-high heat. Add the chanterelles and the remaining salt and pepper and toss them in the butter for about 1 minute just to heat them through; do not overcook.

Heat 1 inch of vegetable oil in a large heavy skillet to 375°F. on a deep-frying thermometer. Fry the 12 tortillas one at a time, holding them with tongs, just until tender, about 10 seconds; pat them dry on paper towels. Cover them with a kitchen towel to keep them moist and warm.

Place a plain tortilla in the center of each large warmed serving plate. Spoon the sauce on top of the tortilla, overlapping its bottom edge. Place 2 filets on top of each tortilla, overlapping the bottom edge, and scatter the chanterelle slices on top. Place a branded tortilla on top of the filets and serve immediately.

Sorrel Sauce
1 tablespoon unsalted butter
2 medium shallots, coarsely chopped
6 bunches sorrel, stemmed and coarsely chopped
½ teaspoon salt
½ teaspoon white pepper
1½ cups Veal Stock (page 212)

Enchilada of Filet Mignon with Chanterelles
12 corn tortillas
12 3-ounce filets mignons
1 teaspoon salt
1 teaspoon black pepper
2 tablespoons vegetable oil
2 tablespoons unsalted butter
1 pound fresh chanterelle mushrooms, washed and cut lengthwise into ¼-inch slices
Vegetable oil for deep frying

Veal Liver Sauté with Cornichons and Jalapeño Vinegar Sauce

This entree is very much in the style of French country cooking. In place of the red wine vinegar a French cook would use, I've substituted jalapeño vinegar for a piquant Southwestern touch.

Buy the highest quality veal liver you can find. It should be creamy rose in color and firm in texture. If you like, have your butcher cut it for you into the thin serving slices called for in the recipe.

TO SERVE 6

Jalapeño Vinegar Sauce
1 tablespoon unsalted butter
1 large shallot, finely chopped
½ cup Jalapeño Vinegar (page 203)
1½ cups Veal Stock (page 212)

Veal Liver Sauté with Cornichons
2¼ pounds veal liver, cut into 6 ⅓-inch-thick slices
½ teaspoon salt
½ teaspoon black pepper
½ cup all-purpose flour
3 tablespoons vegetable oil
½ teaspoon unsalted butter
2 large Cornichons (page 204), cut into ¼-inch dice

For the Jalapeño Vinegar Sauce: Melt the butter in a medium saucepan over moderate heat. Add the shallot and sauté until tender, about 2 minutes. Add the vinegar, bring it to a low, rolling boil, and reduce it by half, about 5 minutes. Stir in the stock and simmer the sauce for about 10 minutes more.

For the Veal Liver Sauté: While the sauce is simmering, prepare the liver. Season it with salt and pepper. Spread the flour on a large plate and dredge the liver slices in the flour.

Heat the oil in a large skillet over moderate-to-high heat. Add the liver in a single layer without crowding, in batches if necessary. Sear the slices for 2 minutes on one side; then reduce the heat to moderate, turn them over and cook for 3 more minutes, until medium-rare.

Remove the liver slices from the skillet and keep them warm. Pour any remaining oil from the skillet. Melt the butter in the skillet and sauté the diced cornichons for about 1 minute, until warmed.

Pass the sauce through a sieve and spoon it into each center of large warmed serving plates. Place a slice of liver on top and sprinkle each serving with diced cornichons.

Texas Longhorn Steer with Vichyssoise Sauce and Red Chile Pesto

The Texas longhorn steer, brought to the Southwest by Spanish settlers, was the first breed of cattle to be raised in North America. Once considered nearly extinct, it is now being raised again commercially, and the rich, deep-red meat is available from some gourmet butchers. If you can't locate longhorn steer, use any good tenderloin cut (filet mignon).

TO SERVE 6

For the Vichyssoise Sauce: Melt the butter in a small saucepan over moderate heat. Add the leeks and sauté until tender, 3 to 5 minutes. Add the potatoes and sauté about 5 minutes more. Add the chicken stock, salt and pepper, raise the heat and simmer the vegetables until the potatoes are tender, 15 to 20 minutes. Transfer the stock and vegetables to a processor and process until smoothly pureed. Pulse in the cream, sieve the sauce and return it to the pan.

For the Texas Longhorn Steer: Preheat the grill or broiler. Season the fillets with salt and pepper and brush them with oil. Oil the grill or broiler pan and cook the steaks about 3 inches from the heat, 5 minutes per side for medium-rare.

While the steaks are cooking, warm the sauce over low-to-moderate heat. Spoon the sauce into the middle of each large warmed serving plate and place 2 steaks side by side on top. Serve the Red Chile Pesto as a condiment in a separate dish.

Vichyssoise Sauce
1 tablespoon unsalted butter
2 medium leeks, white part only, split lengthwise, washed thoroughly and cut into ¼-inch slices
1 large russet potato, peeled, cut into 1-inch cubes, rinsed thoroughly and dried
½ cup Chicken Stock (page 211)
½ teaspoon salt
½ teaspoon white pepper
½ cup heavy cream

12 4-ounce fillets Texas longhorn steer
1 teaspoon salt
1 teaspoon black pepper
1 tablespoon vegetable oil
Red Chile Pesto (page 206)

Rabbit with Lentil Sauce
Served with a Pineapple-Cilantro Salsa

Rabbit is a very home-style dish in the Southwest, and lentils make it even more regional. Sparking the flavors of the meat and sauce is an unusual salsa based on fresh pineapple.

TO SERVE 6

◤ Lentil Sauce

½ cup green lentils, washed
1 ounce smoked bacon, cut into ½-inch pieces
1 small garlic clove, finely chopped
1 teaspoon salt
1 teaspoon white pepper
1 quart water
¾ cup heavy cream

◤ Rabbit

3 rabbits, cut to give 2 hind legs and 2 saddle fillets each
1 teaspoon salt
1 teaspoon black pepper
2 tablespoons vegetable oil
Pineapple-Cilantro Salsa (page 205)

For the Lentil Sauce: Put the lentils, bacon, garlic, salt, pepper and water in a medium saucepan. Bring to a boil over moderate-to-high heat, then reduce the heat and simmer until the lentils are soft, about 30 minutes. Set the lentils aside.

For the Rabbit: Preheat the oven to 400°F. Season the rabbit saddle fillets and legs with salt and pepper. Heat the oil in a heavy ovenproof skillet over moderate heat. Add the saddle fillets and sauté them on 1 side until golden, about 2 minutes; then reduce the heat to moderate-to-low, turn them over and sauté until they are done medium, about 3 minutes more. Remove the fillets from the skillet, set them aside and keep them warm. Raise the heat back to moderate, add the legs to the skillet and sauté them until golden on 1 side, about 3 minutes; then turn them over and put the skillet in the oven. Bake the legs until medium-to-well done—about 10 minutes. Juices should run clear when legs are pierced with a thin skewer.

While the legs are roasting, put ¾ cup of the cooked lentils with their liquid into a processor with the cream. Process until smoothly pureed, then heat the sauce over moderate heat for about 3 minutes.

Spoon the lentil sauce into the center of each large warmed serving plate. Mound 4 tablespoons of the salsa on each plate, on top of the lentil sauce. Rest the thigh end of a rabbit leg on the salsa. Slice each saddle fillet at a 45-degree angle into ½-inch-thick slices and fan them across the other side of the plate.

Tenderloin of Pork with Mole Sauce and Gorditas

Mole is a descendant of thick chile-seasoned sauces enjoyed by the Aztec and Mayan civilizations. Though chiles still give the sauce its distinctive fire, mole is noteworthy for another ancient Mayan ingredient: chocolate. A small quantity of unsweetened chocolate gives the sauce in this recipe a luxuriously rich taste and smooth texture that perfectly complement the pork.

TO SERVE 6

For the Mole Sauce: Put the tomatoes, jalapeños, garlic, peanuts, salt and spices in a food processor and process them until smoothly pureed.

Heat the peanut oil in a heavy, medium-size saucepan over moderate-to-high heat. Add the puree from the processor and sauté it, stirring continously, for about 1 minute. Add the stock, bring it to a boil, then reduce the heat and simmer gently until the sauce has reduced to 1½ cups and is thick enough to coat a wooden spoon, about 45 minutes.

For the Gorditas: Preheat the oven to 425°F. Wrap the Gorditas in a sheet of aluminum foil and bake them for 10 minutes to heat them through.

For the Tenderloin of Pork: As soon as the Gorditas go into the oven, prepare the pork. Season the pork tenderloins with salt and pepper. Heat the oil in a large ovenproof skillet over high heat. Add the tenderloins and sear them for 2 minutes on each side; then put the skillet in the oven and cook for about 6 minutes more, until the tenderloins are cooked medium-well.

Just before serving, stir the chocolate into the sauce until it melts and pass the sauce through a sieve. Spoon the mole in the middle of each of 6 large warmed serving plates. Cut each tenderloin into 6 diagonal slices and arrange them along 1 side of each plate. Unwrap the gorditas and place 3 along the other side of each plate.

Mole Sauce

6 large ripe tomatoes, peeled and seeded
5 green jalapeño chiles, roasted, peeled, stemmed and seeded (page 22)
4 medium garlic cloves, peeled
¾ cup blanched raw peanuts, roasted in a 425°F. oven for 5 minutes
1 teaspoon salt
½ teaspoon ground cinnamon
¼ teaspoon ground coriander
¼ cup peanut oil
3 cups Veal Stock (page 212)
3 ounces bitter chocolate, coarsely chopped

18 Gorditas (page 196)

Tenderloin of Pork

6 tenderloins of pork, about 6 ounces each
½ teaspoon salt
½ teaspoon black pepper
2 tablespoons vegetable oil

Pasta "Burritos" of Ham Mousse with Mustard Sauce and Fresh Sage

Burritos are basically a casual dish of flour tortillas wrapped around a filling. I've taken the concept and turned it into an elegant entree—ham mousse encased in green chile pasta. Mustard and sage go wonderfully with the smoky flavor of the ham.

TO SERVE 6

For the Burritos: Put the coarsely chopped ham, bread crumbs, egg, cream, sage, salt and pepper in a processor and process until smoothly pureed. Remove the puree from the processor and fold in the diced ham.

Roll out the pasta with your pasta machine or by hand into 2 thin strips, each about 4 inches wide and 15 inches long. In a large, shallow saucepan, bring 2 quarts of water to a full, rolling boil with 2 tablespoons of kosher salt and 1 tablespoon of vegetable oil. Add the strips of pasta and cook them until tender but still slightly chewy (al dente) about 3 minutes.

Lay 2 long sheets of plastic wrap, long edges toward you, on a work surface. Drain the pasta strips and place them along the sheets of plastic. Spoon the ham mousse mixture along the center of each noodle, from one end to the other. Fold the edge of each noodle closest to you over the mousse; then fold the other edge over the first to enclose the mousse completely, and roll the filled noodles over so their seam sides are down.

With a very sharp knife, trim the ends of both filled noodles on a diagonal. Then diagonally cut each strip into 3 pieces, to make 6 "burritos." Place the burritos, seams down, on a buttered baking sheet and set them aside.

For the Mustard Sauce: Melt the butter in a medium saucepan over moderate-to-high heat. Add the shallots and sauté them until soft, about 2 minutes. Add the cream, bring it to a boil, then reduce the heat and cook the cream at a low, rolling boil until it has reduced by half, about 25 minutes. Stir in the mustard, sieve the sauce, and keep it warm.

While the sauce is reducing, preheat the oven to 425°F. Cover

◣◻ *Pasta Burritos of Ham Mousse*

2¼ pounds good-quality cooked smoked ham, half coarsely chopped, half cut into ¼-inch dice
1 cup fine egg bread crumbs
1 egg
3 tablespoons heavy cream
6 fresh sage leaves, or 1 teaspoon dried sage
½ teaspoon salt
½ teaspoon white pepper
1¼ pounds Green Chile Pasta (page 202)
2 tablespoons kosher salt

◣◻ *Mustard Sauce*

1 tablespoon unsalted butter
3 shallots, coarsely chopped
3 cups heavy cream
¼ cup extra-strong Dijon mustard
12 fresh sage leaves, for garnish

Pasta "Burrito" of Ham Mousse with Mustard Sauce and Fresh Sage

the burritos with a damp kitchen towel and bake them until heated through, about 10 minutes.

Spoon the sauce into the center of each large warmed serving plate. With a spatula, transfer a burrito to the center of each plate. Place a pair of sage leaves, stems crossed, at 1 side of the plate overlapping the sauce.

Saddle of Lamb with Tortilla Lasagna and Tomato Chile Sauce

Lasagna, broadly defined, is any dish of wide noodles layered with fillings and baked. I've extended the definition by replacing the noodles with flour tortillas and filling them with goat cheese and basil. I serve my "lasagna" along with a spicy fresh tomato sauce as an accompaniment to sliced rare saddle of lamb.

TO SERVE 6

▼⌐ Tomato Chile Sauce
3 tablespoons olive oil
3 large garlic cloves, finely chopped
1 medium onion, coarsely chopped
1 teaspoon dried oregano
1 cup dry white wine
9 medium-size ripe tomatoes, seeded and coarsely chopped
2 teaspoons tomato paste
1 teaspoon chile pequín (available in Latin markets)
1 teaspoon sugar
½ teaspoon salt
½ teaspoon black pepper

▼⌐ Tortilla Lasagna
3 flour tortillas
10 ounces aged creamy goat cheese
½ cup coarsely chopped fresh basil

For the Tomato Chile Sauce: Heat the oil in a large saucepan over moderate-to-high heat. Add the garlic, onion and oregano and sauté until the garlic and onion are tender, about 2 minutes. Add the wine, bring it to a boil, and reduce it by half, about 10 minutes. Then add the tomatoes, tomato paste, chile, sugar, salt and pepper. Cook the sauce at a bare simmer until it has reduced by half, about 40 minutes. Sieve the sauce and keep it warm.

For the Tortilla Lasagna: While the sauce is reducing, prepare the lasagna. Preheat the oven to 425°F. and bake the tortillas until slightly dry but not crumbly, about 1 minute. Place a tortilla on your work surface. Spread on half of the cheese and sprinkle it with half of the basil; place the second tortilla on top, spread it with the remaining cheese, and top it with the remaining basil; cover with the third tortilla.

With a large, sharp knife, cut the layered tortillas into 6 wedges, and trim off the curved sides of the wedges to make 6 triangles. Place the "lasagna" triangles on a lightly buttered baking sheet and loosely cover them with foil. Bake them until heated through, about 10 minutes.

Saddle of Lamb with Tortilla Lasagna and Tomato Chile Sauce

◣▭*Saddle of Lamb*

2 whole boned loins of lamb,
  about 1 pound each after
  boning
½ teaspoon salt
½ teaspoon black pepper
2 tablespoons vegetable oil

For the Saddle of Lamb: As soon as the lasagna goes into the oven, prepare the lamb. Season the saddles with the salt and pepper. Heat the oil in a medium ovenproof skillet over moderate-to-high heat. Add the saddles, fat side up, and saute them for 1 minute; then turn them over and put them into the oven for 8 minutes more, to cook them medium-rare.

Drain the lamb saddles on paper towels. Cut each saddle into 3 equal pieces, and cut each piece vertically into 4 or 5 slices.

Spoon the sauce along the bottom half of each large warmed serving plate and arrange the lamb slices on top. Place a portion of tortilla lasagna on the top half of the plate.

CHAPTER 8

DESSERTS

Chocolate Truffle Antelope Torte with Caramel Lime Sauce

I decorate this giant flat chocolate truffle, served in wedges like a torte, by dusting cocoa powder over a stencil based on a Southwestern native antelope or deer motif. Try drawing and cutting out your own antelope stencil. Or make an abstract pattern from thin strips of waxed paper, or thick clear plastic, laid across the truffle's surface.

Use a good quality Belgian or French chocolate rich in cocoa butter. At Saint Estèphe, I use the French brand Guittard.

TO SERVE 6

⊒☞ Chocolate Truffle Torte

¾ cup heavy cream
10 ounces dark semisweet chocolate, broken into ½-inch pieces
1½ tablespoons unsweetened cocoa powder

⊒☞ Caramel Lime Sauce

1 cup sugar
1 tablespoon water
¾ cup heavy cream
½ cup fresh lime juice

For the Chocolate Truffle Torte: Line an 8-inch circular cake pan with a large circular coffee filter or a circle of waxed paper large enough to come halfway up the pan's side.

In the top of a double boiler place the cream and chocolate pieces and stir until the chocolate has melted completely and is fully blended with the cream.

Pour the mixture into the lined cake pan and chill it in the refrigerator until solid, at least 2 hours. To unmold the truffle, place a circle of cardboard or a flat plate over the pan. Dunk the bottom of the pan in warm water, then invert it turning it out onto the cardboard or plate. Lift off the pan and peel off the paper.

Place a decorative stencil on top of the truffle. Hold a small, fine sieve over the truffle's surface and spoon the cocoa powder into the sieve. Gently tap the sieve as you move it around above the truffle to dust its surface evenly. Carefully lift off the stencil. Store the truffle in the refrigerator until serving time.

For the Caramel Lime Sauce: Put the sugar and water in a heavy medium-sized skillet. Heat the mixture over moderate heat, stirring frequently, until the sugar melts and turns a medium caramel color, 10 to 15 minutes.

Immediately add the cream and stir until it is fully incorporated. Remove the pan from the heat. Then stir in the lime juice and let the sauce cool to room temperature.

To serve the truffle, spoon some of the sauce into the middle of each chilled dessert plate. Cut a wedge of the truffle and place it on top of the sauce.

Chocolate Truffle Antelope Torte with Caramel Lime Sauce

SAINT ESTÈPHE'S MOLDED CHOCOLATE DESSERTS

The two recipes that follow are among the most popular Southwestern-style desserts at Saint Estèphe: Chocolate Chiles Rellenos and White Chocolate Corncobs, the first made from dark chocolate, the second from white, shaped in large chile- or corncob-shaped molds, filled with nut-flavored buttercreams and served with complementary sauces. Elaborate though they seem, these lavish chocolates can be made at home if you follow some simple guidelines.

Use the best-quality chocolate you can find, a variety with a high cocoa-butter content. Never melt the chocolate in a pan over direct heat, as it scorches easily. Instead, melt the chocolate in a double boiler: break it into small pieces or shavings, place them in a small saucepan, and rest the bottom of the pan inside a larger pan filled with water heated to just below boiling point. Be careful not to splash water into the chocolate, which will cause it to stiffen.

A process known as "tempering" is the key to producing chocolate that can be molded successfully. Simply put, tempering is a controlled method of melting chocolate so that its fat content and cocoa solids do not separate and the chocolate stays smooth and shiny. Well-tempered chocolate also unmolds easily with a light tap of the mold against the work surface.

To temper dark chocolate: Melt half of the chocolate in a double boiler, stirring it with a wooden spoon, until it reaches 113°F. on a candy thermometer. Stir in the remaining chocolate and bring the temperature of the melted chocolate down to 82°F., lifting the pan out of the water or returning it to the water as necessary to control the temperature. With the pan again over the water, stir the chocolate until it reaches 88°F. At this point, it is tempered and ready to pour into molds.

To temper white chocolate: Follow the same procedure as for tempering dark chocolate, but heat it to an initial temperature of 110°F. When you stir in the remainder, bring the chocolate down to 80°F.; then bring the temperature back up to 86°F.

Our chocolates at Saint Estèphe are custom-made for us by Mary Yoon at

Entiché du Chocolat, in Whittier, from molds designed by me and manufactured by Doug Parrish, a local expert on vacuum molds. You can use any decorative chocolate mold of your choice, purchased from a good kitchen-supply or confectioner's-supply store; metal molds should be nickel-plated, and plastic molds should be polycarbonate, to ensure easy unmolding. If you want chile or corncob molds, and cannot find them, write to me at Saint Estèphe for further details.

Dark Chocolate Chiles Rellenos with Hazelnut Buttercream and Coffee Crème Anglaise

The chile, a hallmark of Southwest cuisine, finds it way onto the dessert menu at Saint Estèphe in the form of these chocolate chiles rellenos made in chile-shaped molds.

TO SERVE 6

Prepare the Coffee Crème Anglaise and set it aside.

For the Dark Chocolate Chiles Rellenos with Hazelnut Buttercream: Melt and temper the chocolate, following the method described on the preceding page. Pour the chocolate into 6 6-inch by 1-inch chile-shaped chocolate molds, one at a time, turning the molds to coat them evenly and adding enough chocolate for a coating about ⅛ inch thick. Leave them at cool room temperature until the chocolate is set, about 20 minutes.

Meanwhile, prepare the buttercream filling. Preheat the oven to 400°F. Spread the hazelnuts on a baking sheet and roast for 5 minutes. Remove the nuts from the oven and, when they are cool enough to handle, rub them between a pair of kitchen towels to remove their skins. Not every bit of skin will come off. Put them in a processor and pulse the machine until they are chopped to a coarse meal.

Beat the egg yolks with an electric beater until they are thick and lemon-colored and form a ribbon when the beater is lifted out.

Bring the sugar and water to a boil in a small heavy saucepan and continue boiling until they reach the hard-ball stage—about

Coffee Crème Anglaise
¼ recipe Crème Anglaise (page 213), made with 2 tablespoons ground espresso coffee added to the milk with the vanilla bean

Dark Chocolate Chiles Rellenos with Hazelnut Buttercream
½ pound bittersweet chocolate
½ cup shelled hazelnuts
8 egg yolks
½ cup sugar
½ cup water
1¾ cup unsalted butter, softened

Chocolate Indian Paint
3 ounces bittersweet chocolate, coarsely chopped
½ teaspoon vegetable oil

250°F.—on a candy thermometer. With the electric beater running, slowly pour the hot sugar syrup into the egg yolks; continue beating until the yolks cool, about 5 minutes. Then gradually beat in the butter, stopping when the buttercream is smooth. Stir in the chopped hazelnuts.

When the chocolate rellenos are firmly set, unmold them by gently tapping the molds against the work surface. Carefully spoon the buttercream filling into the rellenos and smooth the tops.

Spoon the Coffee Crème Anglaise onto chilled serving plates. Place a chocolate chile filled side down on top of the Coffee Crème Anglaise at one side of each plate.

For the Chocolate Indian Paint: Melt the chocolate with the vegetable oil and put it in a plastic squeeze bottle. Paint a pair of zigzags on the other side of the plate.

White Chocolate Corncobs with Almond Buttercream, Caramel Sauce and Mango Kernels

TO SERVE 6

▤☞ *White Chocolate Corncobs with Almond Buttercream*
½ pound white chocolate
½ cup blanched almonds
8 egg yolks
½ cup sugar
½ cup water
1¾ cup unsalted butter, softened

▤☞ *Mango Kernels*
1 ripe mango, peeled, seeded and cut into ¼-inch dice
1 tablespoon lemon juice
½ teaspoon sugar

▤☞ *Caramel Sauce*
1 cup sugar
1 tablespoon water
¾ cup heavy cream

continued

For the White Chocolate Corncobs with Almond Buttercream: Melt and temper the white chocolate, following the method described on page 174. One at a time, pour the chocolate into 6 6-inch by 1-inch corncob-shaped chocolate molds, turning the molds to coat them evenly and adding enough chocolate for a coating about ⅛ inch thick. Leave them at cool room temperature until the chocolate is set, about 20 minutes.

Meanwhile prepare the buttercream filling. Preheat the oven to 400°F. Spread the almonds on a baking sheet and roast for 5 minutes. Remove them from the oven. When they are cool, transfer the nuts to a processor and pulse until they are chopped to a coarse meal.

Beat the egg yolks with an electric beater until they are thick and lemon-colored and form a ribbon when the beater is lifted out.

Bring the sugar and water to a boil in a small heavy saucepan and continue boiling until they reach the hard-ball stage, about 250°F. on a candy thermometer. With the electric beater running,

Top: Dark Chocolate Chile Relleno with Hazelnut Buttercream and Coffee Crème Anglaise. Bottom: White Chocolate Corncob with Almond Buttercream, Caramel Sauce and Mango Kernels

6 dried corn husks (available at Latin markets; or use husks from fresh ears)

slowly pour the hot sugar syrup into the egg yolks; continue beating until the yolks cool, about 5 minutes. Then gradually beat in the butter, stopping when the buttercream is smooth. Stir in the chopped almonds.

When the cobs are firmly set, unmold them by gently tapping the molds, hollow sides down, against the work surface. Carefully spoon the buttercream filling into the corncobs and smooth the tops. Set them aside in a cool place.

For the Mango Kernels: Toss the mango dice together with the lemon juice and sugar in a small bowl; cover and chill in the refrigerator for at least 30 minutes.

For the Caramel Sauce: Put the sugar and water in a heavy medium-sized skillet. Heat the mixture over moderate-to-high heat, stirring frequently until the sugar melts and turns a medium caramel color, 10 to 15 minutes. Immediately add the cream and stir until it is fully incorporated. Remove the pan from the heat and let the sauce cool to room temperature.

To serve the corncobs, tear a thin strip from the edge of each corn husk and use it to tie one side of the husk to form a boat shape. Place a chocolate corn cob inside each husk boat with its stem end near the knot; place the husk with the cob in the middle of a chilled serving plate. Spoon the sauce inside the husk and around it on the plate. Sprinkle diced mango kernels over the sauce.

Gâteau Rothschild with Cactus Pear Coulis

This French-style cake of chopped almonds and chocolate flakes is typically served with a sharp-flavored sauce—usually a raspberry coulis. I serve it with a coulis of cactus pears, which provides the perfect contrasts of taste and color.

TO SERVE 6

For the Cactus Pear Coulis: Puree the cactus pears in a processor, then press them with a rubber spatula or a large spoon through a fine sieve to remove their seeds. Transfer the puree to a small saucepan, stir in the sugar and lemon juice, and bring the mixture to a boil over moderate-to-high heat. As soon as it boils, remove the mixture from the heat and transfer it to a bowl. Let the coulis cool to room temperature, then chill it in the refrigerator for at least 30 minutes.

For the Gâteau Rothschild: Put the ladyfingers in a processor and process them to a fine powder. Remove them to a mixing bowl. Put the almonds in the processor and pulse the machine until they are coarsely chopped, about the size of lentils. Add them to the ladyfingers and stir in the baking powder. Set the mixture aside.

Break the chocolate into several pieces and put it in the processor. Pulse the machine until the chocolate is chopped to the size of small chips. Set the chopped chocolate aside in a separate bowl.

In another bowl, stir together the sugar and butter until smoothly blended; then stir in the eggs until they are fully incorporated. Gradually stir in the ladyfinger-and-almond mixture, then stir in the chocolate.

Preheat the oven to 325°F. Grease and flour a 9-inch round cake pan and line it with parchment paper or waxed paper. Pour the batter into the pan and bake the cake until it is golden brown and springs back when its center is touched, 30 to 40 minutes.

Let the cake cool in the pan. Then unmold it onto a flat plate or a circle of heavy cardboard and peel off the paper. Cut out thin strips of paper in Southwestern-style zigzags, steps or arrows, and lay them across the top of the cake. Hold a small sieve above the surface of the cake and spoon the powdered sugar into the sieve; gently tap the sieve and move it in a circle to dust the cake evenly. Carefully lift off the strips of paper to leave a decorative pattern.

To serve, spoon some of the Cactus Pear Coulis onto chilled individual dessert plates. Cut wedges of the Gâteau Rothschild and place them on top of the coulis.

Cactus Pear Coulis

5 ripe cactus pears, peeled and sliced
¼ cup sugar
3 tablespoons lemon juice

Gâteau Rothschild

20 ladyfingers
½ cup blanched almonds
½ teaspoon baking powder
3½ ounces bittersweet chocolate, chilled
⅔ cup sugar
5 tablespoons unsalted butter, softened
3 eggs
2 tablespoons powdered sugar

Blue Cornmeal Crepes with Pumpkin Ice Cream and Grapefruit Grand Marnier Sauce

Blue cornmeal is such an important staple in the Southwestern kitchen that it finds its way into every course, even dessert. Here it is paired with another local ingredient, pumpkin, and refined into a very elegant recipe, one of the most popular desserts on the menu at Saint Estèphe.

TO SERVE 8

≡☞ Pumpkin Ice Cream
1 small pumpkin (about 2 pounds)
1 quart Crème Anglaise (page 213)

≡☞ Blue Cornmeal Crepes
1 cup finely ground blue cornmeal
1 cup milk, plus some extra to thin batter if necessary
2 eggs
½ cup sugar
6 tablespoons unsalted butter, melted

≡☞ Grapefruit Zest Garnish
Zest of four grapefruits, peeled with a zester or vegetable peeler
1 cup water
½ cup sugar
¼ cup lemon juice

≡☞ Grapefruit Grand Marnier Sauce
½ cup sugar
1 cup fresh grapefruit juice
½ cup Grand Marnier

For the Pumpkin Ice Cream: Preheat the oven to 350°F. Cut the pumpkin in 1-inch-wide slices, leaving the rind on, and place them in a baking dish or roasting pan. Bake for about 45 minutes, until flesh is tender. Spoon the cooked flesh from the rind and puree it in a processor. Put the puree in a saucepan over low heat and cook it, stirring frequently, until all liquid evaporates, about 10 minutes. Stir 1 cup of the puree into the Crème Anglaise and freeze the mixture in an ice-cream machine.

For the Blue Cornmeal Crepes: Stir together the cornmeal, milk, eggs, sugar and 2 teaspoons of the melted butter, to make a light, creamy batter; if it is too thick, stir in a little more milk. Heat a 6-inch omelet pan over moderate-to-low heat, lightly brush with some of the remaining melted butter, and pour in about 3 tablespoons of the batter; turn the pan to evenly coat its bottom, and pour out excess batter. Cook the crepe for about 1 minute, until its edges start to brown and curl; then turn it with a spatula and cook 45 seconds more. Stack the crepes between pieces of waxed paper to keep them moist. Continue until you have 16 crepes.

For the Grapefruit Zest Garnish: Put the zests in a small saucepan with the water, sugar and lemon juice and cook over moderate heat until the zests are candied and coated with a thick syrup, about 10 minutes.

For the Grapefruit Grand Marnier Sauce: Put the sugar in a small heavy saucepan over moderate heat and caramelize it, stirring occasionally, until golden brown, about 10 minutes. Stir in the

Top: *Blue Cornmeal Crepes with Pumpkin Ice Cream and Grapefruit Grand Marnier Sauce.* Bottom: *Grandma Eloisa's Empanaditas*

grapefruit juice and Grand Marnier and simmer until the sauce is reduced by about half, to ¾ cup, and is thick and syrupy. Cool to room temperature.

To *assemble the dessert*: For each serving, place 2 crepes half overlapping on a large plate. Place a scoop of ice cream at the center of each crepe. Spoon about 4 tablespoons of the sauce around the edges of the crepes and decorate the ice cream with the grapefruit zest and its syrup. Serve immediately.

Grandma Eloisa's Empanaditas

Empanada is the Spanish word for "breaded," and has come to mean a filled pastry turnover all over Latin America. Empanaditas are *little* turnovers, and nobody makes them better than my Grandma Eloisa in Santa Fe. This is her recipe. She uses a completely authentic Southwestern filling that is very similar to the original mincemeat made centuries ago in England in that it actually includes meat. But the combination of pine nuts, sugar, fruits and spices that are mixed with the meat in the filling result in a very special dessert pastry that, like mincemeat, is a favorite at Christmas. At Saint Estèphe, we serve empanaditas with Anise Ice Cream, a nice complement to the hot, crisp pastries.

The quantities that follow make many more pastries than you would serve at a sit-down dinner, but Grandma Eloisa never makes just a few of anything. The empanaditas freeze well, either uncooked or already fried. Just increase the frying time by a few minutes when you cook frozen, unfried empanaditas, or reheat already fried ones in a 400°F. oven for about 12 minutes.

TO MAKE ABOUT 5½ DOZEN

The Filling

1 pound pork butt, trimmed and cut into ½-inch cubes
¾ cup sugar
⅓ cup unsweetened apple sauce

For the Filling: Put the pork butt cubes in a saucepan and add enough water to cover completely. Bring the water to a boil, reduce the heat, and briskly simmer the pork until it is very tender, about 1½ hours.

Drain the pork well and, as soon as it is cool enough to handle, pick the cubes apart into shreds with your fingers. Put the shreds of meat into a mixing bowl and stir them together with the remaining filling ingredients. Set the filling aside.

For the Pastry: Cream together the lard and sugar. With your fingertips, work in the flour until the mixture resembles coarse meal. Stir in just enough of the water to make a firm, not-too-moist dough. Knead the dough until smooth.

On a floured board, roll out the dough as thinly as possible—no more than ⅛-inch thick. With a 3-inch round cookie or biscuit cutter or an inverted glass, cut it into circles.

To assemble the empanaditas, put about 2 teaspoons of the filling in the center of each circle of dough. Dip your finger in water and moisten the rim of each circle. Then fold the circle over the filling and seal the edges together by pressing them down with the tines of a fork.

Heat several inches of oil in a deep fryer or large heavy skillet to a temperature of 400°F. Fry 6 to 10 empanaditas at a time for about 3 minutes, turning them over once, until golden brown. Drain them well on paper towels and pat them dry. For dessert, serve 2 or 3 empanaditas per portion, arranged at the top of the plate with 2 scoops of Anise Ice Cream at the bottom.

⅓ cup pine nuts, toasted (page 24) and coarsely chopped
¼ cup seedless raisins, coarsely chopped
2 teaspoons cilantro seed, ground in a spice mill or coffee grinder
¼ teaspoon allspice
¼ teaspoon cinnamon
¼ teaspoon powdered cloves
¼ teaspoon powdered ginger

The Pastry
2½ tablespoons lard
1 teaspoon sugar
⅓ cup all-purpose flour
4 to 6 teaspoons cold water

Vegetable oil for deep frying
Anise Ice Cream (page 183)

Anise Ice Cream

Star anise gives this ice cream a finer, purer flavor than you would get from licorice extract or a sweet anise-flavored liqueur.

TO MAKE ABOUT 1 QUART

Combine the milk, ½ cup of the sugar and the crushed anise in a medium saucepan. Put the pan over moderate-to-high heat and stir constantly until the milk is just scalded.

Beat together the remaining sugar and the egg yolks with an electric or hand beater until the mixture is thick enough to form a ribbon when the beater is lifted out.

With a whisk, beat the egg-yolk mixture into the milk mixture. Continue cooking, stirring constantly with a wooden spoon, until the mixture is thick enough to coat the spoon. Remove the pan from the heat and stir in the cream.

2 cups milk
1 cup sugar
3 tablespoons star anise, coarsely ground in a mortar or spice mill
6 egg yolks
1 cup heavy cream

Pour the mixture through a fine sieve set over a medium-sized metal bowl to remove the particles of star anise. Fill a large bowl with ice and rest the metal bowl inside, stirring occasionally until the mixture has cooled to room temperature. Transfer the mixture to an ice-cream maker and freeze it according to instructions.

Abiquiu Valley Apricot Ravioli with Yerba Buena Crème Anglaise

As a young boy, one of my favorite outings was the early fall visits we took each year to my Aunt Corina and Uncle Gabriele's ranch in the Abiquiu Valley, about 35 miles north of Santa Fe. Their riverbank orchards yielded plump golden apricots, which were later made into enough chunky preserves to supply the whole family. We ate those wonderful preserves all year, and a taste of them would bring back memories of those cool, damp orchards.

I first made these dessert ravioli with a jar of Abiquiu Valley apricot jam. And now this modern recipe, no matter where the apricots I use come from, is linked to those childhood memories. As a sauce for the ravioli, I first used a classic Crème Anglaise. But the taste of the Abiquiu Valley demanded something more Southwestern. I've since added fresh mint, known as *yerba buena*—"the good herb."

TO SERVE 6

Apricot Ravioli

½ cup coarsely chopped dried apricots
6 tablespoons ricotta cheese
¼ cup Grandma Eloisa's Apricot Preserves (page 208 or recipe of your choice)
1½ pounds Egg Pasta (page 201)

For the Apricot Ravioli: Put the dried apricots, cheese and preserves in a processor and pulse a few times, just until they are well combined but still fairly coarse-textured.

Roll out the pasta as thinly as possible and let it dry (page 200). Trim the pasta to 12 even 4- by 5-inch rectangles. With a pizza cutter or a crinkle-edged ravioli wheel, cut each rectangle into 4 equal 1- by 1¼-inch rectangles. Place about 2 teaspoons of the apricot filling in the center of each of 24 of the rectangles. Dip your finger in water and moisten the edges of the rectangles, then place one of the remaining rectangles on top of each. Press

Abiquiu Valley Apricot Ravioli with Yerba Buena Crème Anglaise

☞ *Yerba Buena Crème Anglaise*

2 cups Crème Anglaise
(page 213)
¼ cup coarsely chopped fresh
mint

¼ cup pine nuts, toasted
(page 24)
3 whole fresh apricots
(optional, if in season),
halved and pitted
6 sprigs fresh mint

down around the edges with your fingers, then trim the edges slightly with the cutter or ravioli wheel to ensure a tight seal. Set the ravioli aside.

For the Yerba Buena Crème Anglaise: Prepare 2 cups of the Crème Anglaise and stir it together with the mint in a medium saucepan over very low heat. Cook, stirring occasionally, for about 10 minutes, until the mint is tender. Remove the sauce from the heat. Whisk the sauce or pulse it briefly in a processor, then sieve it to remove the pieces of mint, and keep it warm.

In a medium saucepan, bring 2 quarts of water to a rolling boil with 1 tablespoon of sugar. Add the ravioli and cook them for about 6 minutes, until the pasta is translucent. Remove the ravioli with a slotted spoon and drain them on paper towels.

Spoon the sauce into the middle of each large warmed serving plate and place 4 ravioli on top. Garnish each plate with a scattering of pine nuts and a fresh apricot half (if available) with a mint sprig tucked in the stem end.

Cactus Pear Granité

Granités, literally grainy ices, are served in many French restaurants as a palate cleanser and refresher before the main course. At Saint Estèphe, I like to make a granité in the traditional French way, only I use a fruit of the desert that has refreshed Southwestern natives for centuries.

TO SERVE 6

4 ripe cactus pears, peeled and
sliced (about 1 cup)
2 tablespoons sugar
2 tablespoons lemon juice
Dry vermouth

Puree the cactus pears in a processor, then press them with a rubber spatula or a large spoon through a fine sieve to remove their seeds. Put the puree in a shallow 5- by 7-inch baking pan. Stir in the sugar and lemon juice and put the pan in the freezer.

Every 15 minutes, remove the pan from the freezer, stir up the puree with a fork, and return the pan to the freezer. When the puree resembles light, grainy ice crystals (about 1 to 1½ hours, depending on the coldness of your freezer), the granité is ready to serve. Spoon it into chilled champagne glasses and add a splash of vermouth to each serving.

Cactus Pear Granité, Yerba Buena Lime Sorbet, and Grapefruit Tequila Sorbet

Yerba Buena Lime Sorbet

The flavor of fresh mint leaves, *yerba buena*, makes this an especially cooling sorbet.

===

TO SERVE 6

1 quart fresh lime juice, strained
¾ cup sugar
¼ cup coarsely chopped fresh
  mint leaves
Fresh mint sprigs, for garnish

Put the lime juice, sugar and mint in a medium saucepan over moderate-to-high heat. Bring them to a boil, stirring continuously; then immediately remove the pan from the heat.

Let the liquid cool to room temperature. Pour it through a strainer to remove the mint leaves, then transfer it to an ice-cream maker and freeze it according to the manufacturer's instructions. Serve in chilled glasses or dishes, garnished with sprigs of fresh mint.

Grapefruit Tequila Sorbet

Make this sorbet in the fall, when pink grapefruit are at their sweetest.

===

TO SERVE 6

1 quart fresh pink grapefruit
  juice, strained
½ cup light tequila
½ cup sugar

Stir together the grapefruit juice, tequila and sugar, until the sugar has dissolved.

Transfer the mixture to an ice-cream maker and freeze it according to the manufacturer's instructions. Serve in chilled glasses or dishes.

Poached Red Indian Peaches with Nougat Sauce

All over the Southwest, red Indian peaches usher in the last days of Indian summer in early October, and to me they have the same fine sweetness of those last warm days. Their blushing skin and flesh gives this dessert a special beauty, but you can use any large, ripe, juicy freestone peaches. In either case, this is a charming dish.

TO SERVE 6

For the Poached Red Indian Peaches: Put the sugar in a large saucepan with 2 quarts of water and bring to a boil over moderate-to-high heat. Reduce the heat to maintain a bare simmer and add the peaches. Poach them until tender, about 8 minutes. Remove them with a slotted spoon to drain upside down on a rack.

For the Marzipan Leaves and Stems: With your hands, knead together 8 tablespoons of the almond paste with the powdered sugar, ½ of the egg white, and the green food coloring, until it is evenly colored, soft and smooth. Place the green marzipan between 2 sheets of waxed paper and roll it out to a thickness of about ⅛ inch. Remove the top sheet of paper and, with the tip of a small sharp knife, cut 12 leaves, about 2 inches long, out of the marzipan. With the tip of the knife, indent a vein down the center of each leaf. Set the leaves aside.

Knead the remaining tablespoon of almond paste together with the remaining ½ of the egg white and the cocoa powder. Shape the brown marzipan by hand into 6 stem shapes and set them aside.

For the Buttercream Filling: Beat the egg yolks with an electric beater until they are thick and lemon-colored and form a ribbon when the beater is lifted out.

Split the vanilla beans in half lengthwise and, with the tip of a knife, scrape the seeds into the beaten egg yolks.

Bring the sugar and water to a boil in a small heavy saucepan and continue boiling until they reach the hard-ball stage, about 250°F. on a candy thermometer. With the electric beater running, slowly pour the hot sugar syrup into the yolks.

Continue beating until the yolks cool, about 5 minutes; then gradually beat in the butter, stopping when the mixture is

1 cup sugar
6 ripe red Indian peaches, washed and stemmed

Marzipan Leaves and Stems
9 tablespoons almond paste or marzipan (buy a good commercial variety)
¼ cup powdered sugar
1 egg white
3 drops green food coloring
½ tablespoon unsweetened cocoa powder

Buttercream Filling
8 egg yolks
2 large vanilla beans
½ cup sugar
½ cup water
¾ pound unsalted butter, at room temperature

Apricot Glaze
2 tablespoons Grandma Eloisa's Apricot Preserves (page 208 or apricot preserves of your choice)
1 tablespoon Grand Marnier

continued

Nougat Sauce

1 cup shelled hazelnuts
1 cup sugar
1 tablespoon water
1 cup Crème Anglaise (page 213), chilled

smooth. Spoon the finished buttercream into a piping bag with a narrow tip.

With a pair of needle-nosed pliers, carefully reach down through the stem opening of each peach and get a firm grip on the pit; pull the pit out, taking care not to damage the peach. Pipe the buttercream into the peaches. Place the peaches right side up on the wire rack.

For the Apricot Glaze: Warm the apricot preserves and Grand Marnier in a small saucepan over moderate heat, stirring just until the preserves liquefy, 2 to 3 minutes. Pass them through a sieve. Brush the glaze over all the peaches to coat them lightly. Tuck 2 marzipan leaves into the stem opening of each peach, and place a marzipan stem in the center. Chill the peaches in the refrigerator while you make the Nougat Sauce.

For the Nougat Sauce: Preheat the oven to 400°F. Spread the hazelnuts on a baking sheet and roast them for 5 minutes. Remove them from the oven and, when they are cool enough to handle, rub them between a pair of kitchen towels to remove most of their skins.

Put the sugar and water in a small heavy saucepan over moderate heat. Bring to a boil and continue boiling, stirring constantly, until the syrup turns a golden caramel color, about 10 minutes. Add the hazelnuts to the syrup and pour out onto a buttered baking sheet, carefully spreading the hot mixture with a narrow spatula. Set the sheet aside.

When the caramel-nut mixture has hardened, break it into 1-inch pieces (about) and put them into a food processor. Pulse the machine until the pieces have broken up into coarse granules the size of lentils. Stir the pieces into the chilled Crème Anglaise.

Spoon the sauce into the middle of each large chilled serving plate. Place a peach in the center.

Poached Red Indian Peach with Nougat Sauce

Neon Tumbleweed with Bizcochitos

Sometimes it's surprising where the inspiration for a recipe will come from.

In 1984, one of the dishes I was working on was my version of the nouvelle "dialogue of fruits," a plate thinly coated with a variety of fresh fruit purees and sometimes served as a palate cleanser between courses. I wanted to serve mine as a light, refreshing dessert, something a lot less formal and more fun than the French version.

That's as far as my thinking on the dish had gone at the time I flew to New York that fall to accept an award from *The Cook's Magazine* as one of fifty people in its "Who's Who of Cooking in America." A couple of days after the ceremony, I went with some friends to visit the Museum of Modern Art. While looking at a Jackson Pollock painting, the idea struck me. His abstract swirling pattern of paints reminded me of New Mexican tumbleweeds. Why didn't I swirl the bright fruit purees onto a plate with plastic squeeze bottles like a sort of neon, Jackson Pollock-style tumbleweed?

The dessert still needed something else to make it complete, an earthier texture and taste to complement the smooth, sharp purees. I decided to include a simple *bizcochito*, an anise-and-vanilla-flavored Mexican Christmas cookie. The best ones I know are made by my Grandma Eloisa. When I went home to Santa Fe for Thanksgiving, I asked her for her recipe. On a Sunday morning, with High Mass blaring in Spanish from her radio, I watched as she made them for me, taking notes as she threw them together without using measuring spoons or cups. I decided to cut out Grandma Eloisa's cookie dough with a cactus-shaped cutter (available in many well-stocked kitchen supply stores). It's a shape that looks good with a tumbleweed.

TO SERVE 6

4 cups fresh blackberries
4 cups fresh raspberries
6 kiwis, peeled
1 papaya, peeled and seeded
4 tablespoons lemon juice
4 tablespoons sugar
1 banana
1 pineapple, peeled and cored
Bizcochitos (page 194)

In a processor, separately puree 2 cups each of the blackberries and raspberries, and all of the kiwis and the papaya, adding 1 tablespoon of the lemon juice and 1 tablespoon of the sugar just before each puree is perfectly smooth. With a rubber spatula or large spoon, press each of the berry purees separately (to remove seeds) through a fine sieve into separate bowls. It is not necessary to sieve the other purees. Chill the purees in the refrigerator for at least 1 hour.

Put each of the purees into its own plastic squeeze bottle.

Neon Tumbleweed with Bizochitos

Squeeze the purees onto chilled serving plates in a free-form swirling pattern.

Cut the banana and pineapple into geometric pieces and randomly place them and the reserved blackberries and raspberries on each plate. Serve with cactus-shaped Bizcochitos.

Bizcochitos

1½ cups sugar
1 cup unsalted butter
1½ cups all-purpose flour
1½ teaspoons anise seed
1 teaspoon baking powder
2 eggs
1 teaspoon brandy
½ teaspoon vanilla
Granulated sugar, for sprinkling
Cinnamon, for sprinkling

TO MAKE ABOUT 30 COOKIES

Cream together the sugar and butter just until well mixed. Sift together the flour, anise seed and baking powder and stir them into the sugar and butter, then gently stir in the eggs, brandy and vanilla to make a smooth dough. Chill the dough in the refrigerator for several hours.

Preheat the oven to 375°F. Roll the dough out to a ¼-inch thickness on a lightly floured board. Cut with a cactus-shaped cookie cutter, liberally sprinkle the cookies with sugar and cinnamon, and place them on a baking sheet lined with parchment paper. Bake the bizcochitos for about 10 minutes, or until lightly browned.

CHAPTER 9

THE SOUTHWEST PANTRY

Posole

Posole is one of my favorite foods. In the Southwest, it is frequently served as a side dish. I like to integrate it into other recipes such as the Posole Consommé with Foie Gras and Truffle (page 52).

TO MAKE ABOUT 3 CUPS

1 cup dried posole
6 ounces smoked bacon, cut into 1-inch chunks
3 large garlic cloves, peeled
½ small onion, finely chopped
2 sprigs fresh oregano

Rinse the posole under cold running water. Put it in a bowl, cover it with cold water, and leave it to soak overnight.

Drain the posole and rinse again. Put it in a medium saucepan with the remaining ingredients and 4 quarts of water. Bring to a boil over low-to-moderate heat, skimming occasionally; then simmer the posole gently until it is puffed and tender, about 3½ hours, adding more water as necessary to keep the posole covered.

Remove and discard the bacon, garlic and oregano, and serve. To store the cooked posole, let it cool to room temperature, then refrigerate it, covered. It will keep for up to 5 days.

Gorditas

The name means "little fatties," a nice description for these small, thick flour tortillas.

TO MAKE ABOUT 3 DOZEN

2 cups all-purpose flour
1 teaspoon baking powder
¼ teaspoon salt
1 teaspoon lard, softened
¾ cup lukewarm water

In a mixing bowl, stir together the flour, baking powder and salt. With your fingertips, rub the lard into the dry ingredients. Slowly stir in the water, then knead the mixture briefly to make a smooth, firm yet pliable dough. Cover the dough with a kitchen towel and let it rest for about 30 minutes.

Divide the dough into balls the size of walnuts. On a floured work surface, roll out the balls one at a time with a floured rolling pin to a thickness of about ⅛ inch.

Heat a griddle over moderate-to-low heat. Cook the gorditas until dark brown blisters form on their undersides, about 30 seconds; then turn them over and cook about 30 seconds more. Wrap them in a towel to keep them warm.

Blue Cornbread

While the blue cornmeal in this recipe has a stunning visual impact, the cornbread will also be good made with yellow cornmeal. You can vary the recipe by adding ¾ cup of fresh corn kernels to the batter.

You can also bake the cornbread in cast-iron corncob pans, available in many gourmet kitchen stores; the quantities below will make about 30 large cobs. Bake the cornbread cobs for 15 to 20 minutes. I like to present the cobs individually wrapped in fresh green corn husks.

TO MAKE 2 9-BY-14-INCH PANS

Preheat the oven to 325°F.

Sift together the cornmeal, flour, sugar, baking powder and salt. In a separate bowl, stir together the butter, egg and milk; gradually stir them into the dry ingredients.

Spoon the batter into 2 buttered 9-by-14-inch cake pans. Bake the cornbreads for 25 to 30 minutes, until firm and springy to the touch and lightly browned.

1 cup blue cornmeal
1 cup all-purpose flour
3 tablespoons sugar
1½ teaspoons baking powder
½ teaspoon salt
⅓ cup butter, melted
1 egg, beaten
1 cup milk

Tortilla Chips

You can make fresh tortilla chips from blue or gold corn tortillas. But be sure to use *thin* tortillas, particularly if they are blue ones, to ensure that your chips will be light and crisp.

TO SERVE 6

Cut each tortilla into 6 wedges.

Heat several inches of oil in a deep fryer or a large, deep, heavy skillet to a temperature of 425°F. on a deep-frying thermometer. Fry the tortillas in 4 batches until very crisp but not yet browned, about 45 seconds per batch.

Drain the chips well on paper towels and serve them warm, sprinkled with salt if desired.

12 blue or gold corn tortillas
Vegetable oil for deep frying
Salt (optional)

Sopaipillas

These large, puffy triangle-shaped "sofa pillows" of deep-fried pastry, a favorite New Mexican treat, make an excellent accompaniment to hors d'oeuvres, main courses or desserts. Traditionally, they are punctured and filled with a spoonful of rich dark honey.

TO MAKE 20 TO 24 SOPAIPILLAS

2½ cups all-purpose flour
  2 tablespoons baking powder
  1 teaspoon salt
  1 teaspoon lard or shortening
  1 cup warm milk
    Vegetable oil for deep frying

In a large mixing bowl, stir together 2 cups of the flour with the baking powder and salt. Add the lard and rub it into the dry ingredients with your fingertips. Add the milk and work it in by hand, gradually adding enough of the remaining flour to make a soft but dry dough that comes away from the bowl and can be gathered together in a ball. Knead the dough for a few minutes until smooth. Cover the dough with a kitchen towel and let it rest for about 45 minutes.

With your hands, roll the dough on a floured board into an even rope about 1 inch thick. Cut the rope in half. Keeping the board lightly floured, roll out ½ of the rope with a rolling pin to make a long rectangle about ¼ inch thick and 3 inches wide. With a long, sharp knife, cut the rectangles into triangles with sides about 4 inches long. Place the triangles in single layers between sheets of waxed paper. Repeat with the second half of the rope.

Heat several inches of oil in a deep-fat fryer or large heavy skillet to a temperature of 375°F. on a deep-frying thermometer. Drop a few triangles of dough at a time into the hot oil. They will sink to the bottom, then gradually rise to the surface. Keep pushing them under with a slotted spoon or wire skimmer as they gradually puff up. Fry them for 1 to 1½ minutes, turning them once, until golden. Drain them on paper towels and serve hot on individual plates or in a towel-lined basket.

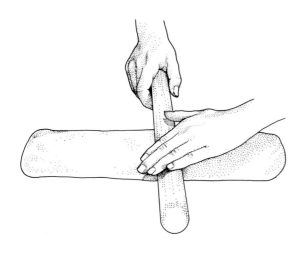

BASIC PASTA TECHNIQUE

I use a classic Italian home-style technique to make fresh pasta, mixing the dough directly on the work surface with an ordinary table fork. All of the recipes listed below use the same basic techniques for mixing the dough, kneading it, rolling it out and drying it. But doughs will behave somewhat differently, depending on their ingredients—some of them drier and harder to knead, others moister and more fragile to roll out. The important thing in every case is to trust your hands to tell you how the dough feels and when it is ready to go on to the next stage of preparation.

At Saint Estèphe, we make our pasta with an ordinary small Atlas hand-operated pasta machine that clamps to the edge of a kitchen counter or table. This type of pasta machine is widely available at a modest cost, and is very easy to use. I prefer the consistency of handmade pasta to the softer pasta made from expensive electric machines that mix and extrude the dough automatically.

All of the recipes that follow will give you a fairly large quantity of dough, enough for several meals. The dough keeps so well that it makes sense to prepare more than you need at any one time, so you have pasta ready whenever you decide to prepare a recipe.

Mixing and Kneading the Dough

Sift together the dry ingredients into a mound directly on the work surface. Make a well in the center, right down to the work surface, and break the eggs directly into the well, adding any other moist ingredients that are called for in the recipe as well.

With a fork, begin to beat the eggs vigorously, gradually incorporating the dry ingredients from around the inner rim of the well; cup your other hand and gradually push in the outer rim of the dry ingredients as they are incorporated into the pasta dough. When most of the dry ingredients have been incorporated, use a spatula or scraper to mix the dough, scraping it up from the work surface and folding it over to blend it evenly. If the dough seems too wet, sprinkle in a little more flour as you work the mixture; if too dry, add a little more oil or another egg, as called for in the recipe.

Gather the dough up and lightly flour the work surface. Knead the dough, repeatedly pressing it down and away with the heel of your hand, then folding it over and giving it a quarter-turn. Sprinkle on a little more flour as necessary if the dough is wet and sticky, or add a little oil if it is too dry. Continue kneading just until the dough is smooth, firm and elastic, with no stickiness, 3 to 5 minutes.

At this stage, the dough can be stored if desired. Gather it into a ball and wrap it in waxed paper. Then wrap it securely in plastic wrap. The dough will keep for several weeks in the refrigerator, or may be frozen for several months. Let the dough return to room temperature before continuing.

Rolling the Dough

Divide the dough into large handfuls, and work with a handful at a time. Flatten and smooth the handful of dough into a flat circle the same width as the roller on your pasta machine.

Set the rollers on the machine to their widest width. Lightly flour both sides of the dough circle and roll it through the machine. Fold the dough in half, flour it, and roll it through again, continuing the process until the dough is fairly dry, elastic and smooth and no longer breaks up or comes through the rollers looking at all patchy.

Then decrease the roller width by 1 setting, rub a little flour into both sides of the dough, and pass it through unfolded. Continue decreasing the settings, rubbing the sheet of dough with flour and rolling it through, cutting the sheet in half when it gets too long to handle easily.

The end result should be a fairly thin sheet of pasta (at the setting of "5" on the Atlas machine). A perfectly rolled sheet of pasta could be described as feeling as soft, smooth and dry as a piece of chamois cloth.

Drying the Dough

Drape the sheets of pasta on a drying rack, or over a broom handle resting between 2 chair backs. Leave them for about 20 to 30 minutes, until fairly dry but still flexible. Pasta can also be prepared in advance to this stage, with the individual sheets stacked, after drying, on a plate between sheets of waxed paper, then covered with plastic wrap and refrigerated.

Egg Pasta

This basic pasta dough makes excellent ravioli, which I stuff with either Ravioli of Carne Adobada as an appetizer (page 80) or apricots and ricotta in Abiquiu Valley Apricot Ravioli (page 184).

TO MAKE ABOUT 1 POUND

Mix and knead the dough following the basic pasta techniques given above, adding the butter to the well with the eggs. For ravioli, roll out the dough as thinly as the pasta machine will allow, or roll it out as thinly as possible with a rolling pin on a floured board. Dry the dough as described above.

2½ cups high-gluten bread flour
4 eggs
½ teaspoon butter, softened

Red Chile Pasta

Red chile powder gives this pasta an earthy, brick-red color and a flavor that, though distinctive, is not overwhelmingly spicy. Sieving the powder before mixing the dough removes large particles of chile, resulting in a finer pasta. The chile powder makes the dough fairly dry and a little more resistant to rolling out than an ordinary egg dough, but patience and persistence will give you good results. The number of eggs used in the dough will vary depending on humidity and on how dry or absorbent your chile powder and flour are.

TO MAKE ABOUT 2½ POUNDS

Sift together 2 cups of the flour and the chile powder and mound them on the work surface. Make a deep well in the center, down to the work surface. Break 4 of the eggs into the well and add the oil.

Mix and knead the dough following the basic pasta techniques given above, adding 1 or 2 more eggs if the dough gets too dry. Then roll it out and dry it as directed above, and cut the dough as called for in the specific recipe.

2 to 2½ cups high-gluten bread flour
2 cups sieved red chile powder
4 to 6 eggs
1 tablespoon vegetable oil

Green Chile Pasta

Green chiles alone won't give pasta dough an intense green color. At Saint Estèphe we prepare a simple chlorophyll extract of fresh parsley and spinach to color our green chili pasta dough. Without actually altering its flavor the extract gives the pasta a color as vibrant as its jalapeño chile flavor. The chlorophyll extract and the chiles tend to make the mixture fairly moist, so you'll find yourself working in extra flour as you knead and roll the dough.

TO MAKE ABOUT 2½ POUNDS

3 bunches fresh parsley, washed and dried
3 bunches fresh spinach, washed and dried
12 pickled whole jalapeño chiles, stemmed and seeded
5 to 6 cups high-gluten bread flour
4 eggs
1 tablespoon vegetable oil

Put the parsley and spinach in a processor or blender and process them to a fine puree. Strain the puree through a double thickness of fine cheesecloth or a linen napkin (use an old one—it will be permanently stained) over a bowl, bunching and twisting the puree inside the cloth to extract as much green liquid as possible. Reserve the liquid and discard the pulp.

Put the green liquid in a medium skillet over low heat. Within 4 or 5 minutes, a layer of dark green chlorophyll solids will rise to the surface; skim off and keep the solids, and discard the thin liquid underneath.

Put the chlorophyll in a processor with the chiles and process until finely pureed.

Mound 5 cups of the flour on the work surface and form a well in its center. Add the chlorophyll and chile mixture, the eggs and oil. Mix and knead the dough following the basic pasta techniques given above, adding more flour if the dough is too moist and sticky. Then roll it out according to the basic preparation described above, working in more flour as necessary to prevent the dough from breaking up in the pasta machine. Dry the dough, then cut it as called for in the specific recipe.

Blue Cornmeal Pasta

Blue cornmeal produces pasta with a striking pale blue-gray color, a hearty texture and a pronounced corn flavor. The relative coarseness of the cornmeal is reduced a little by processing and sieving it first, and a large quantity of egg whites in the recipe gives the dough greater smoothness (reserve the egg yolks for another use). But you'll still find that the dough is harder to roll out thinly than other pasta doughs; stop rolling a notch or two sooner on your machine, and just cook the slightly thicker noodles a few minutes longer than you ordinarily would. The recipe is also excellent made with yellow cornmeal instead of blue.

TO MAKE ABOUT 3 POUNDS

2½ cups blue cornmeal
2½ cups semolina flour
3 whole eggs
11 egg whites
¼ to ½ cup cold water

Process the cornmeal in a processor for about 1 minute, then pass it through a fine sieve to remove any large particles. Sift together the cornmeal and flour and mound them on the work surface. Make a deep well in the center, down to the work surface. Break the eggs into the well, and add the egg whites and ¼ cup of the water.

Mix and knead the dough following the basic pasta techniques given above, adding more of the water if the dough gets too dry. Then roll it out and dry it as directed above, and cut the dough as called for in the specific recipe.

Pickled Chiles in Jalapeño Vinegar

This recipe serves two distinctive purposes in the Southwest pantry. The pickled chiles make a very piquant garnish, as in the Duck Liver Mousse with Bouquet of Pickled Chiles in Aspic (page 39). And the white wine vinegar in which they are pickled becomes, after several days, a spicy Jalapeño Vinegar, wonderful to use in sauces and dressings.

3 fresh green jalapeño chiles
3 fresh red jalapeño chiles
3 fresh yellow jalapeño chiles
3 fresh green serrano chiles
3 fresh red serrano chiles
2 long green Anaheim chiles
1 whole garlic clove, peeled
1 whole shallot, peeled
½ teaspoon salt
6 whole black peppercorns
1 quart white wine vinegar

Wash the chiles and put them in a clean glass jar with the garlic, shallot, salt and peppercorns. Bring the vinegar to a boil in a medium saucepan and pour it over the chiles and seasonings, covering them completely.

Let the vinegar cool for about 2 hours, then cover the jar and store it in a cool, dark place. The chiles and vinegar will be ready to use in 6 to 8 days.

Cornichons Pickled with Green Chiles

Cornichons, the French term for baby cucumbers, make wonderfully crisp, tart pickles. Buy the smallest springtime cucumbers you can find—2 inches or less is an ideal size—picked before they ripen.

5 pounds baby cucumbers
3 fresh green Anaheim chiles, sliced in half lengthwise
6 garlic cloves, peeled
6 bay leaves
2 quarts white wine vinegar
1 cup kosher salt
1 tablespoon whole black peppercorns

Pack the cucumbers, chiles, garlic and bay leaves into 3 sterilized 1-quart pickling jars.

Put the vinegar, salt and peppercorns in a medium saucepan and bring to a boil over high heat, stirring to dissolve the salt. Pour the hot vinegar mixture over the pickles, filling the jars completely. Cool to room temperature, cover the jars, and store them in a cool, dark place. The pickles will be ready to eat in about 2 weeks, and will keep for about 6 months.

Jalapeño Preserves

Serve this wonderful sweet and spicy jelly as a condiment with hors d'oeuvres. Or use it as an accompaniment to lamb, as you would mint jelly.

TO MAKE ABOUT 4 PINTS

10 fresh jalapeño chiles, stemmed and finely chopped
4 red bell peppers, stemmed, seeded and finely chopped
7 cups sugar
2 cups red wine vinegar
9 ounces liquid fruit pectin

Put the chiles, peppers, sugar and vinegar in a large, heavy saucepan over moderate heat. Bring the mixture to a boil, stirring occasionally, then reduce the heat and simmer for about 15 minutes. Stir in the pectin, raise the heat and, when the mixture returns to a boil, remove the pan from the heat.

Submerge 4 pint-sized canning jars in boiling water and boil them for 15 minutes to sterilize. Drain the jars and fill them with the preserves to about ½ inch from the top. Pour a ⅛-inch layer of melted paraffin on top of the preserves to seal.

When the preserves have cooled and the paraffin has solidified, cover the jars with their lids. Store them in a cool, dark place, where the preserves will keep for up to 1 year.

Pineapple-Cilantro Salsa

In this twist on the usual Southwestern salsa, fresh pineapple replaces the tomato or tomatillo.

TO MAKE ABOUT 3 CUPS

½ medium-size pineapple, peeled, cored and cut into ½-inch cubes
1 small onion, coarsely chopped
1 small garlic clove, finely chopped
1 bunch cilantro leaves, finely chopped
½ teaspoon chile pequín (available in Latin markets)
½ teaspoon salt
¼ teaspoon oregano
¼ teaspoon cayenne pepper

Toss together all the ingredients in a mixing bowl. Cover the bowl and chill the salsa in the refrigerator for at least 1 hour.

Red Chile Pesto

Like a traditional Italian pesto, this sauce is thickened with toasted pine nuts and olive oil. But its flavor and color come from a blend of roasted red chiles and red bell peppers. Serve this rich, hot-sweet sauce as a condiment for grilled meats.

TO MAKE ABOUT 1 CUP

3 fresh red Anaheim chiles, roasted, peeled, stemmed and seeded (page 22)
3 small red bell peppers, roasted, peeled, stemmed and seeded
½ cup pine nuts, toasted (page 24)
¼ cup olive oil
½ teaspoon salt
½ teaspoon white pepper

Put all the ingredients in a processor or blender. Process until they form a thick puree. Serve either at room temperature or chilled.

To store the pesto, put it in a small bowl or jar and smooth its surface. Pour a thin film of olive oil to completely cover it and act as a seal, and put the bowl in the refrigerator. When you use more of the sauce, just stir in the oil, smooth the surface, and add another film of oil. The pesto will keep for up to 10 days.

Gold Corn Preserves

This traditional corn relish makes an excellent side dish for a buffet or hors d'oeuvre party. You can put it up in preserving jars, or just refrigerate it in a covered bowl and use it within 2 weeks.

TO MAKE ABOUT 2 PINTS

1 teaspoon salt
3 cups fresh corn kernels (about 2 large ears)
5½ cups sugar
1½ cups white vinegar
6 ounces fruit pectin
1 small red bell pepper, stemmed, seeded and finely diced

Bring 2 quarts of water with 1 teaspoon of salt to a boil in a medium saucepan. Add the corn kernels and cook them until tender, about 5 minutes. Drain well.

Bring the sugar and vinegar to a boil, stirring frequently, in a medium saucepan over high heat. Add the pectin and when the liquid returns to a boil, remove the pan from the heat. Stir in the corn and bell pepper.

Submerge 2 pint-size canning jars in boiling water and boil them for 15 minutes to sterilize. Drain the jars and fill them with the preserves to about ½ inch from the top. Pour a ⅛-inch layer of melted paraffin on top of the preserves to form a seal.

When the preserves have cooled and the paraffin has solidified, cover the jars with their lids. Store them in a cool, dark place, where the preserves will keep for up to 1 year.

Chayote Chutney

Chayote, an avocado-shaped squash, is very popular in the Southwest. Its mild green flavor goes wonderfully with sugar and spices in this unusual chutney. In India, chutneys are served as condiments along with appetizers and main courses. I like to serve my chutney as one of the accompaniments to a large hors d'oeuvre corncob of fresh cream cheese (Corncob of Queso Blanco, page 41).

TO MAKE ABOUT 2 QUARTS

Put the vinegar, sugar, salt, ginger, allspice and cloves in a large heavy saucepan. Bring them to a boil over moderate-to-high heat. Add the raisins, chiles, onions and lemon juice and zest; reduce the heat and simmer briskly, stirring frequently, until almost all the liquid has been absorbed, about 30 minutes. Add the chayotes and cook, stirring occasionally, for about 30 minutes more.

Store the chutney in a covered jar or dish in the refrigerator, where it will keep for up to 30 days.

3 cups cider vinegar
2 cups brown sugar
2 tablespoons salt
2 teaspoons ground ginger
1 teaspoon ground allspice
1 teaspoon ground cloves
2 cups seedless raisins
6 fresh green Anaheim chiles, stemmed, seeded and coarsely chopped
1 large onion, coarsely chopped
Juice and zest of 1 lemon
3 pounds chayotes, peeled, seeded and cut into ¼-inch dice

Grandma Eloisa's Apricot Preserves

My Grandma Eloisa makes a large batch of these preserves every autumn from the harvest of Aunt Corina and Uncle Gabriele's apricot orchards at Abiquiu.

TO MAKE ABOUT 3 QUARTS

6 cups ripe apricots (about 5 pounds), halved, pitted and trimmed of all blemishes
6 cups sugar
1 large ripe pineapple, peeled, cored and coarsely chopped

Crush the apricots with your hands and put them in a large, heavy saucepan with the sugar. Stir the mixture constantly over moderate-to-high heat until it is very thick, about 30 minutes.

Add the chopped pineapple to the saucepan, reduce the heat to moderate, and continue cooking until most of the juice has evaporated and the mixture is very thick, about 30 minutes more.

To bottle the preserves, pour them while still hot into 6 sterilized pint-sized canning jars, filling the jars to within ½ inch of the rim and smoothing the surface. Pour a ⅛-inch-thick layer of melted paraffin over the preserves. Cool to room temperature, then cover securely and store in a cool, dark place, where the preserves will keep for up to 1 year.

The preserves can also be kept in a covered dish or jar in the refrigerator for up to 2 months.

Basic Mayonnaise

This mayonnaise will keep in the refrigerator in a covered jar for about 2 weeks.

TO MAKE ABOUT 1½ CUPS

6 egg yolks, at room temperature
1 cup vegetable oil, at room temperature
1 tablespoon Dijon mustard
1 tablespoon red wine vinegar
½ teaspoon salt
½ teaspoon white pepper

Put the egg yolks in a processor and process them until they are thick and a lemon-yellow color. With the machine running, pour in the oil in a slow, thin trickle; as the mayonnaise begins to thicken and mount, slowly increase the flow of the oil. When all the oil has been incorporated, turn off the machine. Then add the remaining ingredients and pulse the processor several times until they are thoroughly incorporated.

INDIAN PAINTS

Many of the dishes we serve at Saint Estèphe are decorated with plate "paintings" of Southwestern motifs. For first courses and entrees we use the following three different kinds of "Indian Paints," naturally colored and flavored with red chile, green sorrel and yellow saffron cream; our molded chocolate desserts (page 174) are decorated with melted chocolate. Though it sometimes looks very elaborate, as in the Salmon Painted Desert (page 128), the sauce-painting technique is really fairly simple.

Put the paint in a small plastic squeeze bottle with a fine tip, which can be purchased in kitchen stores; you can even use plastic squeeze bottles from ketchup or mustard. Invert the bottle and shake it gently downward to move all the paint toward the tip for an uninterrupted flow. Holding the tip just above the surface of the plate, gently squeeze the bottle as you move it in the desired pattern.

You might want to experiment with the technique on a paper towel or waxed paper before you use it for finished dishes. With a little practice, you'll be able to paint plates quickly and easily.

Red Chile Indian Paint

TO MAKE ABOUT 1¼ CUPS

Heat the oil in a small skillet over moderate heat. Add the garlic and saute it until tender but not brown, about 3 minutes. Sprinkle in the red chile powder, stirring constantly. Immediately add the water and stir until well blended.

Remove the skillet from the heat and pass the paint through a fine sieve. Store it in the refrigerator until needed.

1 tablespoon vegetable oil
2 medium garlic cloves, finely chopped
½ cup red chile powder, mild to medium-hot
¾ cup water

Green Sorrel Indian Paint

I use jars of pureed sorrel, available from gourmet food stores, for my green Indian paint. When fresh sorrel is available, wash, stem and shred the leaves and sauté them gently in a little unsalted butter. The leaves will dissolve into a puree in a few minutes; continue cooking them, stirring frequently, until the puree is thick and smooth.

TO MAKE ABOUT 1½ CUPS

¾ cup vegetable oil
2 medium garlic cloves, finely
  chopped
¾ cup sorrel puree
1 teaspoon salt
1 teaspoon white pepper

Heat the oil in a small skillet over moderate heat. Add the garlic and sauté it until tender but not brown, about 3 minutes. Stir in the sorrel and seasonings.

Transfer the mixture to a processor and pulse several times until the paint is smoothly blended. Pass the paint through a fine sieve and store it in the refrigerator until needed.

Yellow Saffron Indian Paint

TO MAKE ABOUT 1½ CUPS

1 teaspoon saffron threads
1 cup heavy cream

Crush the saffron threads with your fingertips and put them in a bowl. Stir in the cream. Leave them to soak at room temperature until the saffron has turned the cream a bright yellow, about 1 hour.

Lightly whip the cream to soft peaks. Spoon the paint into a plastic squeeze bottle. Store the paint in the refrigerator until needed.

Fish Stock

TO MAKE ABOUT 2½ QUARTS

Put the fish bones and heads, vegetables, herbs, lemon, peppercorns and water in a large stockpot. Slowly bring the water to a boil over moderate heat, skimming foam from its surface frequently until no more forms.

Simmer the stock until the liquid has reduced by about a third, about 1½ hours. Strain out the solids. Put the stock in a large bowl; let it cool to room temperature, then refrigerate it. Skim any solidified fat from its surface.

The stock will keep well for 8 days in the refrigerator, or up to 30 days in the freezer.

4 pounds fish bones and heads from white-fleshed fish, preferably halibut
2 large onions, peeled and quartered
1 large leek, white part only, cut in half lengthwise
2 bunches parsley
2 bay leaves
1 large lemon, quartered
½ tablespoon whole black peppercorns
4 quarts water

Chicken Stock

TO MAKE ABOUT 2½ QUARTS

Put the chicken carcasses, vegetables, herbs and water in a large stockpot. Slowly bring the water to a boil over moderate heat, skimming foam from its surface frequently until no more forms.

Simmer the stock until the liquid has reduced by about a third, about 1½ hours. Strain out the solids. Put the stock in a large bowl; let it cool to room temperature, then refrigerate it. Skim the solidified fat from its surface.

The stock will keep well for 6 days in the refrigerator, or several months in the freezer.

4½ pounds chicken carcasses (from about 3 chickens)
3 large celery stalks, cut into 2-inch pieces
2 large carrots, cut into 2-inch pieces
1 large leek, cut into 2-inch pieces
1 medium onion, quartered
2 bay leaves
1 bunch parsley
½ teaspoon dried thyme
4 quarts water

Duck Stock

4½ pounds duck carcasses and necks (about 3 ducks)
1 tablespoon unsalted butter
3 large carrots, cut into 2-inch pieces
1 large leek, cut into 2-inch pieces
1 large onion, peeled and quartered
1 bunch parsley
6 juniper berries
4 bay leaves
1 tablespoon dried thyme
5 quarts water

Preheat the oven to 425°F. Put the duck carcasses in a roasting pan and roast them until well browned, about 50 minutes, turning them occasionally.

Melt the butter in a large stockpot over moderate heat. Add the carrots, leek and onion and sauté them for about 10 minutes, stirring occasionally. Add the duck carcasses, herbs and water. Slowly bring the water to a boil over moderate heat, skimming foam from its surface frequently until no more forms.

Simmer the stock, uncovered, until the liquid has reduced by about half, 3½ to 4 hours. Strain out the solids. Put the stock in a large bowl; let it cool to room temperature, then refrigerate it. Skim the solidified fat from its surface.

The stock will keep well for 6 days in the refrigerator, or several months in the freezer.

Veal Stock

4 pounds veal knuckles
1 tablespoon unsalted butter
4 large celery stalks, cut into 2-inch pieces
4 medium tomatoes, skinned, seeded and cut into 2-inch chunks
2 large carrots, cut into 2-inch pieces
1 large leek, cut into 2-inch pieces
1 large onion, peeled and quartered
2 bay leaves
1 bunch parsley
1 teaspoon dried thyme
5 quarts water

Preheat the oven to 425°F. Put the veal knuckles in a roasting pan and roast them until lightly browned, about 50 minutes, turning them occasionally.

Melt the butter in a large stockpot over moderate heat. Add the celery, tomatoes, carrots, leek and onion and sauté for about 10 minutes, stirring occasionally. Add the veal knuckles, herbs and water. Slowly bring the water to a boil over moderate heat, skimming foam from its surface frequently until no more forms.

Simmer the stock until the liquid has reduced by about half, 3½ to 4 hours. Strain out the solids. Put the stock in a large bowl; let it cool to room temperature, then refrigerate it. Skim the solidified fat from its surface.

The stock will keep well for 6 days in the refrigerator, or several months in the freezer.

For concentrated veal stock, boil the stock again until it reduces by half.

Crème Anglaise

This classic dessert cream, which the French call "English cream," is a pourable custard. It makes a rich foundation for ice cream, and a base for dessert sauces such as the Mint Crème Anglaise that I serve with my Apricot Ravioli (page 184).

TO MAKE ABOUT 1½ QUARTS

8 egg yolks
½ cup sugar
I quart milk
I vanilla bean, split lengthwise

Put the egg yolks and sugar in a processor and process them until they are thick enough to form a ribbon when poured. Remove to a large mixing bowl and set the mixture aside.

Put the milk and vanilla bean in a large, heavy saucepan over moderate heat. Heat the milk until just below the boiling point. Stirring constantly, gradually pour the milk into the egg yolk-and-sugar mixture; return the mixture to the pan over moderate heat and continue stirring until the Crème Anglaise is thick enough to coat a spoon. Do not let the sauce boil or it will curdle. Remove the pan from the heat and pass it through a fine sieve; cool in a bowl set over ice. Crème Anglaise may be stored in the refrigerator for up to 4 days.

A Guide to Southwestern Native Artifacts that Appear in Modern Southwest Cuisine

The presentation of the dishes I've developed for *Modern Southwest Cuisine* has been greatly inspired by the patterns of native Southwestern art. I am indebted to Philip Garaway of the Native American Art Gallery in Venice, California, for lending the objects which appear in the photographs on the following pages:

p. 151   Mano (grinding stone), Mogollon culture, central Arizona, circa 1000 A.D.

p. 160   Navajo Teec Nos Pos Rug, northeastern Arizona, circa 1920s–1930s (collection of Diana and David Jacobs).

p. 173   Zuni Polychrome Deer Heartline Ceramic Jar, Zuni Pueblo, northwestern New Mexico, circa 1890s–1900s A.D.

p. 177   Navajo Late Classic Child's Blanket, circa 1870s.

p. 181   Bottom: Pinedale Polychrome Ceramic Bowl, Mogollon culture, north central Arizona, circa 1300–1400 A.D. Top: Four Mile Polychrome Ceramic Bowl, circa 1300–1400 A.D.

p. 187   Mimbres Arrowheads with Wooden Shafts, Mogollon culture, southwestern New Mexico, circa 1000–1150 A.D.

p. 191   Pinto Polychrome Bowl, Salado culture, south central Arizona, circa 1300–1400 A.D.

Index

Credits

I am grateful to the following people and businesses for lending me the serving plates, original artisans' works and other objects that appear in the photographs in this book.

A Singular Place (Jan Peters and Ray Leier), Santa Monica, California, for pieces by the following artists: Rick Davis, hand-painted ceramic cactus platters, page 111; Doug Irish-Hosler, sandblasted painted porcelain vessel, page 75; Chris Spanovich, pit-fired vessels, pages 57, 185; Shaun Weisbach, handblown glass platter, page 45.

Bob's Nursery, Manhattan Beach, California.

The Broadway (Peggy Danielson), Beverly Center, Beverly Hills, California, for the cast-iron cactus mirror frame in the photograph on page 83.

Buddy's (Buddy Wilson), Hollywood, California, for the serving plates and bowls in the photographs on pages 43, 53, 63, 77, 117, 137 and 173.

By Design (Tony Schlarb), Beverly Center, Beverly Hills, California, for serving plates in the photographs on pages 83, 88, 129, 132 and 181.

Flying Foods (Blake Wheeler and Georges Negle), Santa Monica, California.

Geary's (Rita Gold), Beverly Hills, California, for the platters, plates and bowls in the photographs on pages 37, 57, 68, 121, 144, 151, 154, 160, 166 and 191.

Gump's (Shelton Ellis and John Reck), Beverly Hills, California, for the plates in the photographs on pages 75, 88, 105, 134, 140 and 185.

International Garden Center (Sandy Romero and Greg Barth), El Segundo, California.

Keith's Pottery (Mary and Phil LeMasurier), Manhattan Beach, California, for the skull in the photograph on page 45.

Melamed & Company (Robert Melamed and Charlotte Stack), Redondo Beach, California, for the plates in the photographs on pages 79, 123, 147 and 169.

Solobra (Carol Savid), Taos, New Mexico, for the Hispanic rug in the photograph on page 37; and for the free-form frosted glass plate in the photograph on page 187.

Mark Untener, Lakewood, California, for the ceramic bowl on page 159.

About the Author

John Sedlar, thirty-one, is the chef and co-owner of Saint Estèphe in Manhattan Beach, California, about fifteen miles south of Los Angeles.

Trained in the classical French manner under the late Jean Bertranou, the owner-chef of L'Ermitage in Los Angeles, Sedlar has made a successful marriage of French culinary technique and his heritage of American Southwest cuisine.